TABLE OF CONTENTS

NEWMAN COLLEGE
BARTLEY GREEN
BIRMINGHAM B32 3NT
CLASS 302
BARCODE 01117157
AUTHOR ALL

NW15045   SAP   £12·99

Study Guide

for

Baron and Byrne
Social Psychology
Ninth Edition

Prepared by

Bem P. Allen
Gene F. Smith
Western Illinois University

WITHDRAWN

Allyn and Bacon
Boston London Toronto Sydney Tokyo Singapore

N 0111715 7

Copyright © 2000 by Allyn & Bacon
A Pearson Education Company
160 Gould Street
Needham Heights, Massachusetts 02494-2130

Internet: www.abacon.com

All rights reserved. No part of the material protected by this copyright notice
may be reproduced or utilized in any form or by any means, electronic or
mechanical, including photocopying, recording, or by any information
storage and retrieval system, without the written permission of the copyright owner.

ISBN 0-205-29804-4

Printed in the United States of America

10 9 8 7 6 5 4 3 2 1   03 02 01 00 99

HOW TO USE YOUR STUDY GUIDE

We believe your instructor has chosen the best possible avenue to learning all about SOCIAL PSYCHOLOGY 9th Ed. This textbook is the most comprehensive, up-to-date, interesting account of social psychology that is available. If you master the Baron and Byrne book, you will have a useful grasp of social behavior that will benefit you for years to come.

We also believe that this Study Guide will almost certainly guarantee your mastery of the Baron and Byrne test. Not so incidentally, your Study Guide is such a detailed and systematic approach to the text that careful completion of the exercises in the Guide will give you great odds for a high grade in your social psychology course.

The outline that begins each chapter is to help you appreciate the chapter topics. Looking at it will give you a quick reminder of what is in a chapter. There is room for notes next to outline headings. The first step in mastering a chapter of the text is to read over the objectives for the chapter. The next step is to read the chapter. Look over the objectives and do the reading as soon as the chapter is assigned. Read the chapter before going back to the objectives or you may want to consider the objectives as you read.

After familiarizing yourself with text coverage of objectives for a chapter, do the Guide exercises for that chapter. The first exercise is called "There's More Than First Meets Your Eyes." It helps make sense of the figures and graphs in your text. The second exercise is called "Key Terms." The "Key Terms" section allows master of objectives referring to critical concepts. The "Matching" exercise is third. The "Matching" items will allow you to master objectives which refer to simple concepts. For each matching item, all you have to do is match each phrase on the left with one on the right.

Fourth, do the "What's Wrong Here?" exercise. Items for this exercise will help you master objectives that refer to critical statements in the text. Be careful! An item may be partially correct. However, it is a statement that has been "doctored" so that it looks totally correct, but may contain incorrect information. The fifth exercise is "True-False." This tried and true format (pun intended) will allow you to master objectives that refer to straightforward social psychological principles outlined in the text. The sixth and last exercise is "Fill-in-the-Blanks." Also a familiar format, the "Fill-in-the-Blanks" exercise will allow you to master objectives that refer to the central concepts covered in the text.

Each objective is covered in one or more exercises. Answers are conveniently located near each exercise. You can immediately find out how you did on the items for an exercise without having to search through answers all crammed together at the end of the chapter. To help you further, the Study Guide includes text page numbers after the answers to exercise items. Should you not understand an item after seeing its answer, you can look up the corresponding concept in the text.

After you have finished the exercises, you will have learned the objectives. In turn, having learned the objectives, you will have mastered the text, because the objectives "zero in" on every important consideration in the text. The night before the test on text chapters, go over objectives recalling how each is covered in the text. Then respond to the multiple choice items near the end of the chapter (correct answers are given just after the items).

If you want to even further assure yourself that you know the material in the text, for a few randomly chosen objectives turn to the text to see if your recollection of how those objectives are covered in the text is accurate. This last task should give you considerable confidence.

Learning the objectives means that you have mastered the text and that you are ready to "ace" the test. And "ace it" is not too strong a statement. Here's why: each multiple-choice item that tests your knowledge of text material has been directly drawn from an objective. If you follow the steps outlined above, you will have mastered the material in the text and you can't help but do well on the test.

There is another learning mode you could adopt: Really getting inside each chapter, getting to where it's coming from. A set of "Critical Thinking" questions will allow you to penetrate to the heart of each chapter. Answering them will not only give you better odds on the test, it will provide you with the kind of substantive understanding that will survive for years after the course is over.

Oh, by the way, just for fun, each Guide chapter has an additional section called "If You'd Like to Know More." It contains readings from the popular literature on social psychology (for example, PSYCHOLOGY TODAY). For the first time, this edition includes web site addresses where you can easily find fascinating information about social psychology. Each entry in this section has been selected because it is interesting, informative, and enjoyable.

BPA and GFS

1

THE FIELD OF SOCIAL PSYCHOLOGY: HOW WE THINK ABOUT AND INTERACT WITH OTHERS

CHAPTER OUTLINE: GETTING THE OVERALL PICTURE:

Before reading the chapter, it may be helpful to examine the chapter outline. This will give you an idea of what is covered in the chapter and should help you organize your learning and review the material. You can also record notes on text sections under the outline headings for those sections.

I. Social Psychology: A Working Definition

    A. Social Psychology is Scientific in Nature

        1. "But why adopt the scientific approach? Isn't social psychology just common sense?"

            a. The Confirmation Bias: The Temptation to Verify Our Own Views

            b. The Availability Heuristic: Emphasizing What Comes to Mind First

            c. Mood Effects: How We Feel Often Influences the Way We Think

    B. Social Psychology Focuses on the Behavior of Individuals

    C. Social Psychology Seeks to Understand the Causes of Social Behavior and Thought

        1. The Actions and Characteristics of Other Persons

        2. Cognitive Processes

        3. Ecological Variables: Impact of the Physical World

        4. Cultural Context

        5. Biological Factors

    D. Social Psychology: Summing Up

II. Social Psychology: Where It Is Now, and Where It Seems to Be Going

    A. Influences of a Cognitive Perspective

    B. Growing Emphasis on Application: Exporting Social Psychology

    C. Adoption of a Multicultural Perspective: Taking Full Account of Social Diversity

    D. Increasing Attention to the Potential Role of Biological Factors

III. Answering Questions about Social Behavior and Social Thought: Research Methods in Social Psychology

    A. Systematic Observation: Describing the World Around Us

    B. Correlation: The Search for Relationships

    C. The Experimental Method: Knowledge through Systematic Intervention

        1. Experimentation: Its Basic Nature

        2. Experimentation: Two Requirements for Its Success

    D. Interpreting Research Results: The Use of Statistics, and Social Psychologists as Perennial Skeptics

        1. Interpreting Diverse Results: The Role of Meta-Analysis

    E. The Role of Theory in Social Psychology

IV. The Quest for Knowledge and the Rights of Individuals: Seeking an Appropriate Balance

V. Using This Book: A Road-Map for Readers

LEARNING OBJECTIVES: WHAT YOU SHOULD LEARN

As you are reading the chapter, these objectives provide page–by–page questions for you to answer. Answering the objectives should assure that you understand the essential material in the chapter.

1. Understand the definition of social psychology. [4-6]

2. Explain why social psychology is considered to be a "scientific field." [6-7]

3. Examine "common sense" as a source of knowledge in social psychology. [7-8]

4. Explain how errors in our thinking caused by confirmation bias, the availability heuristic, and mood effects often lead us to false conclusions regarding social behavior and social thought. [8-9]

5. Explain why the field of social psychology focuses its study on the behavior of individuals. [9]

6. Describe the five major causes of social behavior and thought: a) the actions and characteristics of others; b) cognitive processes; c) environmental variables; d) cultural context; and e) biological factors. [11-13]

7. Describe the cognitive perspective and understand the three ways in which this perspective is reflected in social psychological research. [14-15]

8. Note the growing emphasis on application. [15]

9. Examine critically the assumption that the findings of social psychology can be generalized across cultures, across gender, and across diverse groups. [15-17]

10. Describe how the biological/evolutionary perspective has been used to explain various aspects of social behavior. [17-18]

11. Describe the use of systematic observation as a research technique, including naturalistic observation and the survey method. [19-20]

12. Why are representative sampling and wording of questions important when using the survey method? [20]

13. Describe how the correlational method is used to examine a hypothesis. [20-21]

14. Understand why a correlation between two variables does not guarantee that the two variables are causally connected. In other words, understand the third variable possibility. [21-22]

15. Describe the basic steps involved when an investigator conducts an experiment, and indicate why experimentation is often considered the preferred method among social psychologists. [23-24]

16. Understand independent and dependent variables in the context of the heat/aggression experiment. [23-24]

17. Explain why it is important that subjects be randomly assigned to groups in an experiment. [24-25]

18. Why is it important to hold factors other than the independent variable constant? Examine experimenter effects and indicate how the experimenter's effect on research participants can be held constant. [25-26]

19. Describe two constraints that sometimes make it impossible to use the experimental method to investigate a research question. [26]

20. How are statistics used to help psychologists interpret their research results? [27]

21. Why are conflicting results sometimes found, and how do replication and meta-analysis help us interpret research results? [27-28]

22. Trace the steps in building a theory, and summarize how theories are used in social psychology. [28-29]

23. Why do social psychologists sometimes deceive their research participants? [30]

24. Describe ethical issues raised by the use of deception, and indicate how informed consent and debriefing help to decrease the potential dangers of deception. [30-31]

25. Summarize favorable and unfavorable reactions reported by research participants who have been deceived. [31]

There's More Than First Meets Your Eyes: Understanding Figures in Your Text

Turn to the figures in your text that are mentioned below and follow the discussion about how the figures can increase you understanding of research and theory.

1. Despite the fact it's illustrated with a cartoon, the point made in Figure 1.10 (page 22) is a central methodological principle in social psychology. Cause-and-effect can only be documented by performing an experiment. When two naturally-occurring events simply occur together there is no guarantee that the two are causally related to each other.

2. Another important methodological principle is illustrated in Figure 1.12 (page 25). The point being made is that independent variables must be manipulated so that there is only one way in which the different levels of this variable are different. If some other factor differs at the same time as the factor of interest, it is impossible to interpret the results of the experiment. The factor varying simultaneously with the independent variable or the independent variable itself may just as well be the actual cause. The two factors are confounded with each other.

3. Figure 1.13 (page 29) describes the role of theory in research. Students often assume that research is able to "prove" whether a theory is true or false. In fact, we merely increase or decrease our confidence in the theory's ideas. And even when we disconfirm predictions made by a theory, most often the ideas expressed by the theory are then modified and subjected to further testing. It is relatively uncommon for a theory to be flat-out rejected.

KEY TERMS: CONCEPTS YOU NEED TO UNDERSTAND

Write out the meaning of the following terms in your own words. Cover the right-hand portion of the exercise until you have finished, then check on the accuracy of your answers by comparing them with the definitions provided.

1. "common-sense knowledge"

the informal information that has accumulated in a variety of ways, but has never been tested by scientific methods and often presents confusing and inconsistent conclusions [7-8]

2. social psychology

scientific field that seeks to understand the nature and causes of individual behavior and thoughts in social situations [6]

3. the experimental method

research approach in which one factor is systematically varied to determine its effects on the subject's behavior [23]

4. independent variable

the factor that is systematically varied in an experiment [23]

5. dependent variable

the aspect of the subject's behavior that is measured by the experimenter to determine if it is affected by the independent variable [23]

6. correlational method

research approach in which two or more variables are measured to determine whether changes in one variable are associated with changes in the second [21]

7. theories

explanatory frameworks developed by scientists to help conceptualize why certain events or processes occur as they do [28]

8. deception methodology

procedure used in experiments which involves withholding information from subjects or sometimes providing false information [30]

MATCHING:

Match each concept on the left side of the next page with an identifying phrase, word or sentence on the right. The answers may be found after the WHAT'S WRONG HERE? section.

A.	opposite of confounding	___ 1.	participants match larger population
B.	common sense	___ 2.	helps eliminate experimenter effects
C.	correlational method	___ 3.	other variables are held constant
D.	representative sampling	___ 4.	statistical technique for combining results across studies
E.	double-blind procedure	___ 5.	informal "everyday" knowledge
F.	meta-analysis	___ 6.	ethical safeguard
G.	debriefing	___ 7.	interpretations individuals make regarding social situations/events
H.	construals	___ 8.	does not allow cause-and-effect conclusions
I.	ecological variables	___ 9.	weather, smells, phases of the moon

WHAT'S WRONG HERE?

For each statement below indicate what needs to be changed in order to make the statement correct. You will find the answers at the end of the exercise, along with pages in the text where you can find more information.

1. Common sense derived from everyday experience is a reliable source of information about social behavior.

2. According to the text's working definition, social psychology is a nonscientific field.

3. The evolutionary perspective asserts that there is no logical reason why persons seeking a mate should show a preference for a physically attractive partner.

4. Social psychologists who apply knowledge about memory, reasoning, and decision making in order to broaden our understanding of various aspects of social thought and behavior are using the evolutionary perspective in their work.

5. Females are just as likely as males to engage in acts of physical aggression.

6. Male trial attorneys show higher levels of testosterone than attorneys working in other areas of law, but female trial attorneys do not show higher levels of testosterone.

7. A researcher using the technique of naturalistic observation should intrude him/herself into the situation as forcefully as possible in order to maximize the validity of the data gathered.

8. If 85% of the respondents to a survey indicate they are satisfied or very satisfied with their jobs, it is a virtual certainty that 85% would say they'd "choose the same job again."

9. If two variables are correlated with each other, it is certain that one is a cause and the other an effect.

10. Experimental methods are always preferred over correlational methods.

11. Most theories in social psychology consist of mathematical equations.

12. If the predictions derived from a theory are not supported by research findings, the only option is to reject the theory.

13. The goal of most social psychological research is to prove that a particular theory of social behavior is true.

14. Social psychologists use deception in their research because they enjoy watching people fall for the false information.

15. Most research participants who learn that they've been deceived in an experiment resent having been fooled.

WHAT'S WRONG HERE? ANSWERS:

1. The insights contained in common sense are often contradictory and sometimes wrong; our informal observations need to be investigated with the systematic methods of social psychology. [7-8]
2. Social psychology is, of course, a scientific field. [6]
3. It is asserted that physical attractiveness serves as a cue indicating good health and thus also indicating reproductive capacity. [12]
4. Memory, reasoning, and decision making are important processes for cognitive psychologists. [14]
5. Males engage in more acts of physical aggression. [17]
6. Trial attorneys, whether male or female, showed higher levels of testosterone than other types of attorneys. [18]
7. The observer tries to remain as unobtrusive as possible so that his/her presence doesn't influence the behavior being observed. [20]
8. In fact, how questions are worded often dramatically influences the answers obtained. [20]
9. It is possible that a third variable is causing the variation in both variables. [21-22]
10. While experimental methods are generally preferred, practical barriers and ethical constraints often make it impossible to conduct an experiment. [26]
11. Most consist of verbal statements, including definitions of basic concepts and statements concerning the relationships between these concepts. [29]
12. Theories are not always rejected; they are sometimes subject to notification [29]
13. A theory can never be "proven" to be true; we merely increase confidence in its accuracy.
14. They use deception because if research participants knew what was being studied, their behavior would often be affected by this. [30]
15. In fact, most research participants do not resent the use of deception. [31]

MATCHING ANSWERS:

1–D [20]; 2–E [26]; 3–A [25]; 4–F [27]; 5–B [7-8]; 6–G [31]; 7–H [11, 14]; 8–C [21-22]; 9–I [11]

TRUE–FALSE:

Indicate whether each of the following statements is true or false. If false, indicate why. Correct answers are found at the end of the exercise.

1. The text asserts that highly advanced fields such as chemistry, physics, and biology are scientific fields and that social psychology doesn't meet the criteria of science.

2. The characteristic which distinguishes science from non science is the topic which is studied.

3. Our judgments about persons we meet are likely to be influenced by the mood we are in when we meet them.

4. Social psychology focuses its study on groups of persons or on society as a whole.

5. McCall (1997) found that the likelihood that students "carded" a stranger before serving them alcohol was not influenced by whether the stranger was attractive or not.

6. Men are more upset and experience stronger feelings of jealousy when their partner commits an act of sexual infidelity compared to an act of emotional infidelity.

7. Like men, women are more upset and experience stronger feelings of jealousy when their partner commits an act of sexual infidelity compared to an act of emotional infidelity.

8. The role of construals in determining social behavior is a topic studied by evolutionary social psychologists.

9. Strong findings in correlational studies provide conclusive evidence that the variables being measured have a cause-and-effect relationship with each other.

10. The preferred method of research by social psychologists has generally been the experimental method.

11. Social psychologists who have obtained advanced graduate degrees do not have to feel constrained by ethical concerns when conducting experimental research.

12. Most social psychologists believe it is permissible to use deception without informed consent and debriefing.

TRUE–FALSE ANSWERS:

1. False; social psychology is a science too. [6-7]
2. False; the adoption of core scientific values and use of scientific methods are the distinguishing features. [7]
3. True. [9]
4. False; social psychology focuses its study on the behavior of individuals. [9]
5. False; physical attractiveness of the stranger did affect whether they were carded. [10]
6. True. [13]
7. False; women are more upset by emotional infidelity. [13]
8. False, construals are important factors according to cognitive social psychology. [14]
9. False; findings with the correlational method are always ambiguous with regard to causality. [21-22]
10. True. [23]
11. False; obviously ethical guidelines apply to all persons conducting social psychology research. [30-31]
12. False; informed consent and debriefing are important and necessary safeguards. [31]

FILL IN THE BLANKS: A GUIDED REVIEW

Mentally fill in each of the blanks in the following section while covering the answers in the margin. Check each answer against the answer in the margin by uncovering as you go along.

1. Our tendency to notice and remember mainly information that lends support to pre-existing views is known as _____.

   the confirmation bias [8]

2. The mental shortcut which misleads us into thinking that those events that are the easiest to bring to mind are necessarily the most common is the _____.

   availability heuristic [8]

3. To say that our behavior toward others is influenced by _____ means that we are affected by the thoughts and interpretations that pass through our minds as we interact with them.

   cognitive processes [9]

4. The organized system of shared meanings, perceptions, and beliefs held by persons belonging to some group is your text's definition of _____.

   culture [11]

5. The view that biological factors play an important role in social behavior is emphasized by social psychologists who adopt the _____ perspective.

   evolutionary [12]

6. The evolutionary process by which biological features and patterns of behavior which help organisms to reproduce become more prevalent in a species over time is called _____.

natural selection [12]

7. Social psychologists who are interested in issues surrounding personal health, the legal process, and social behavior in work settings are reflecting the growing emphasis on the _____ of social knowledge.

application [15]

8. The research procedure in which a researcher carefully observes and records behavior as it occurs in an everyday setting is using the technique of _____.

naturalistic observation [20]

9. When researchers ask large numbers of persons to respond to questions about their attitudes or their behavior, the method of research being used is the _____.

survey method [20]

10. Both the survey method and the method of naturalistic observation simply involve attempts to describe the world as it exists around us and thus are considered to be examples of _____.

systematic observation [19]

11. In order for a survey to accurately reflect the actual opinions of the population being studied, it is important that the persons who participate in the survey be _____ of the larger population.

representative [20]

12. When careful, systematic observation is made of two naturally–occurring variables to determine whether there is a relationship between them, the _____ method is being used.

correlational [21]

13. The factor which is systematically varied by an experimenter is the _____ variable.

variable [23]

14. Behavior that is displayed by the subject and measured by the experimenter is the basis for the _____ variable.

dependent [23]

15. The method of investigation being employed when an investigator systematically varies the independent variable in order to determine its impact on the dependent variable is the _____ method.

experimental [23-24]

16. According to the principle of _____, each person participating in an experiment must have an equal chance of being exposed to each level of the independent variable.

random assignment [24-25]

17. In addition to random assignment of participants to experimental conditions, a second requirement for conducting a successful experiment is that all factors other than the independent variable must be _____.

held constant [25]

18. When factors other than the independent variable are not held constant, it is impossible to tell whether the results are due to the independent variable or the other factors. The problem is that the independent variable is _____ with the other factors.

confounded [25]

19. The research technique in which neither the participants nor the research assistant having contact with the participants knows the hypothesis under investigation is _____ procedure.

double-blind [26]

20. The special forms of mathematics used to evaluate the likelihood that a given pattern of research results occurred by chance alone is _____.

inferential statistics [27]

20. When statistical analysis suggests that the likelihood of obtaining the observed findings by chance is low, the results are described as _____.

significant [27]

22. The statistical procedure in which the results of many different studies are combined mathematically to determine the effects created by an independent variable is _____.

meta-analysis [27]

23. Testable predictions, usually derived from theories, are called _____.

hypotheses [28]

24. The procedure in which potential research participants are provided with as much information as possible about an experiment, prior to their participation, so they can decide whether to participate is called _____.

informed consent [31]

25. The full description of the purposes of the study given participants after they have completed their participation is called _____.

debriefing [31]

MULTIPLE-CHOICE QUESTIONS: A PERSONAL QUIZ

After you have finished reading the chapter and done the other exercises in the STUDY GUIDE, take the quiz found below to test your knowledge. Indicate your answers by circling the letter of the chosen alternative. Check your answers against the answers provided at the end of the exercise.

1. Your text's evaluation of the "informal knowledge found in common sense" as a source of information regarding social behavior is that
   a. it does not contain a kernel of truth.
   b. it conclusively answered most questions of interest to social psychologists before the field was founded.
   c. its wisdom was recognized only after social psychologists confirmed its truth.
   d. there are enough contradictions in its statements to make it an unreliable source of information.

2. What characteristic distinguishes science from non science?
   a. the topics that are studied
   b. the values that are adopted and the methods that are used
   c. whether the investigators hold advanced degrees
   d. whether a physical or a social phenomenon is studied

3. The approach suggesting that many aspects of social behavior are the result of evolutionary processes in which patterns of behavior that contribute to getting one's genes to the next generation are strengthened in a population is
   a. narrative biology.
   b. meta–biology.
   c. sociobiology.
   d. the evolutionary perspective.

4. Representative sampling and wording of questions are important considerations for researchers who conduct studies using
   a. the survey method.
   b. the correlational method.
   c. systematic observation.
   d. experimentation.

5. The double-blind procedure is designed to minimize
   a. external validity.
   b. experimenter effects.
   c. confounding.
   d. unrepresentative sampling.

6. To say that our behavior is influenced by "cognitive processes" means that we are affected by
   a. memories, decision making, and reasoning processes.
   b. heat, noise, pollution, crowding, and weather.
   c. group memberships, along with cultural factors.
   d. inherited aspects of our sensory and cognitive systems.

7. The term that refers to using social psychological insights to help solve practical problems is
   a. cognitive social psychology.
   b. meta-analysis.
   c. theory.
   d. application.

8. Which of the following is *not* one of the changes your text predicts for social psychology in the coming decades?
   a. continued growth in the influence of the cognitive perspective
   b. increased interest in studying diversity and the impact of cultural and ethnic factors on social behavior
   c. increased interest in applying the principles and findings of social psychology
   d. decreased emphasis on the necessity for informed consent and debriefing.

9. An experimenter exposes subjects to systematically varied levels of temperature to determine its effect on aggression. The temperature level is the _____variable.
   a. independent
   b. dependent
   c. intervening
   d. control

10. Studies that have examined the relationship between temperature and aggression have found that
    a. higher temperatures are associated with lower amounts of aggression.
    b. higher temperatures are associated with higher amounts of aggression.
    c. there is no relationship between temperature and aggression.
    d. both warm and cold temperatures are associated with higher amounts of aggression.

11. When the results of an experiment can be generalized to real-life social situations, the experiment has
    a. external validity.
    b. statistical significance.
    c. theoretical relevance.
    d. representative sampling.

12. The opposite of confounding between variables is to
    a. find statistically significant results.
    b. do a correlational study.
    c. vary several factors simultaneously.
    d. hold constant all other factors while varying the independent variable.

13. Two basic requirements must be met in order for a researcher to conduct a successful experiment. These two basic requirements are to
    a. deceive the subjects and confound the independent variables.
    b. randomly assign subjects to the groups and confound the independent variables.
    c. randomly assign subjects to the groups and avoid interactions.
    d. randomly assign subjects to the groups and avoid confounding.

14. If we observe the amount of aggression occurring on particular days and also record the temperature on those days to determine whether aggression and temperature are related, the type of study we are conducting is
    a. field experiment.
    b. correlational study.
    c. case study.
    d. theoretical research.

15. A sophisticated statistical technique for combining results from many experiments in order to reach an overall conclusion regarding the topic they investigate is
    a. correlational strategy.
    b. converging operations.
    c. replication.
    d. meta–analysis.

16. A primary goal of theories is to provide
    a. a description of social behavior.
    b. an explanation of social behavior.
    c. ethical guidelines for researchers.
    d. a summary of previous research in social psychology.

17. Why do social psychologists use deception in their studies?
    a. They want to protect subjects from the harmful effects of learning negative things about themselves.
    b. They know that causal relationships between independent and dependent variables are impossible to establish without deception.
    c. They believe it is sometimes not possible to obtain useful knowledge if subjects know the true purpose of the study.
    d. They know that subjects usually enjoy experiments more when deception is involved.

18. When research participants agree to be in an experiment after being fully informed about what it will involve, they are providing _____; the full description of the procedure given to the research participants at the end of an experiment is called _____.
    a. informed consent; safeguarding
    b. safeguarding; informed consent
    c. safeguarding; debriefing
    d. informed consent; debriefing

MULTIPLE–CHOICE ANSWERS

1. d [7-8]	6. a [14]	11. a [26]	16. b [28]
2. b [7]	7. d [15]	12. d [25]	17. c [30]
3. a [12]	8. d [18; 31]	13. d [24-25]	18. d [31]
4. a [20]	9. a [23-24]	14. b [21]	
5. b [26]	10. b [24]	15. d [27]	

IF YOU'D LIKE TO KNOW MORE: FURTHER SOURCES OF INFORMATION

Rubin, Z. (1983, March). Taking Deception for Granted. PSYCHOLOGY TODAY, 74–75. This critical overview notes that the use of deception remains at a high level among social psychologists, and it argues that the use of deception retards progress.

Rubenstein, C. (1982, July). Psychology's Fruit Flies. PSYCHOLOGY TODAY, 83–84. Do the college students used in so many experiments behave and think like other adults? Rubenstein argues that the answer may be "no."

Rice, B. (1982, February). The Hawthorne Effect: Persistence of a Flawed Theory. PSYCHOLOGY TODAY, 70–74. It is argued that the original Hawthorne effect study was methodologically unsound, but "lazy authors" continue to describe this idea . . . A good case study of how hard it is to disprove an idea.

Rubin, Zick. (1970, December). Jokers Wild in the Lab. PSYCHOLOGY TODAY, 81 ff. A brief introduction to the use of deception in social psychological research, possible ethical implications, and possible alternative methods.

Go to http://www.wesleyan,edu/spn/profs.htm   This is a directory called Home Pages of Social Psychologists. If at any time during the semester you want to look up information about a particular social psychologist, this is a good place to start. The directory contains a list of more than 500 social psychologists' home pages and email addresses.

THINKING CRITICALLY ABOUT THE FIELD OF SOCIAL PSYCHOLOGY

1. Some persons have argued that some aspects of social behavior are best left unstudied. Among these people was former U. S. Senator William Proxmire from Wisconsin, who gained national attention in the 1970s and 1980s when he gave a monthly award to government-supported research projects he deemed a waste of taxpayer dollars. Among the projects given Proxmire's attention was the work of social psychologists Ellen Bersched and Elaine Hatfield on love. In his press release Proxmire stated that "Americans want to leave some things in life a mystery, and right at the top of things we don't want to know is why a man falls in love with a woman and vice versa." Are questions of how people fall in love and how long-term relationships develop worthy of psychological study? Should some topics be placed out of bounds?

2. Keep an eye out for articles in newspapers and magazines that deal with issues raised in this course. In the current chapter, you might be alert to stories that draw conclusions about cause and effect relationships. In the political and social world, many differences of opinion hinge on whether aparticular variable in a correlational relationship is seen as a causal factor or an effect. Why is density of population related to the crime rate? Why is earning power related to obtaining a college degree? Can you think of different explanations for these relationships?

3. Assume you are a sales clerk at a shoe store. Two customers come into the store, and one of them asks for assistance with a broken heel on a shoe. While seemingly wanting help, she rejects whatever suggestions you make. Later you learn that the two customers were actually researchers studying the helpfulness of store clerks, and that the whole incident was a deception so they could observe and record your behavior in this situation. Would you feel that your rights had been violated if you were the clerk in such a study? Would such a study be ethical under current guidelines for research? During the semester, you might occasionally place yourself in the position of research participants and reconsider the ethical questions raised at the end of Chapter 1.

4. If you were a researcher, would you worry that the requirement of informed consent from research participants might influence their behavior? Two research studies have, in fact, suggested that the use of informed consent can change participants' behavior in significant ways. Gardner argued that informed consent changes behavior in environmental stressor research. Gardner's article is in the *Journal of Personality and Social Psychology* (*36*, 628-634). Dill and colleagues argued that human subjects' regulations are a source of methodological artifact. Their study appeared in *Personality and Social Psychology Bulletin* (*8*, 417-425).

5. There are numerous examples where common knowledge simply is not accurate regarding behavior. Perhaps the best examples in social psychology are Milgram's famous studies of obedience to authority figures, found toward the end of the Social Influence chapter. When people are informed of Milgram's procedure and asked to predict the behavior of hypothetical research participants, most people expect a very low level of obedience to the researcher's demand that shocks be delivered to another person. And yet, when ordered to do so, most participants complied with the researcher's requests and delivered the "required" shocks. Does the fact that the average person's predictions are so inaccurate make it a necessity that the research be done?

2 SOCIAL PERCEPTION: UNDERSTANDING OTHERS

CHAPTER OUTLINE: GETTING THE OVERALL PICTURE:

Before reading the chapter, it may be helpful to examine the chapter outline. This will give you an idea of what is covered in the chapter and should help you organize your learning and review the material.

    B. Attribution: Some Basic Sources of Error

        1. The Correspondence Bias: Overestimating the Role of Dispositional Causes

        2. The Actor-Observer Effect: You Fell; I Was Pushed

        3. The Self-Serving Bias: "I'm Good; You're Lucky"

    C. Social Diversity: A Critical Analysis—Cultural Differences in the Self-Serving Bias

    D. Applications of Attribution Theory: Insights and Interventions

        1. Attribution and Depression

        2. Attribution and Rape: Blaming Innocent Victims

III. Impression Formation and Impression Management: How We Combine—and Use—Social Information

    A. Cornerstones of Social Psychology: Asch's Research on Central and Peripheral Traits

    B. Impression Formation: The Modern Cognitive Approach

    C. Impression Management: The Fine Art of Looking Good

        1. Tactics of Impression Management and Their Relative Success

        2. Impression Management: Is It Always a Conscious Process?

    D. The Accuracy of Social Perception: Evidence That It's Higher Than You Might Guess

LEARNING OBJECTIVES: WHAT YOU SHOULD LEARN

As you are reading the chapter, these objectives provide page-by-page questions for you to answer. Answering the objectives should assure that you understand the essential material in the chapter.

1. Explain how information about people's inner states is communicated through the five basic channels of nonverbal communication. Why is this information oftentimes more accurate than verbal communication? [39-40]

2. Describe the six (or perhaps seven) basic emotions expressed in unique facial expressions. Does this mean we are limited to only a small number of facial expressions? [40]

3. Understand Ekman and Friesen's (1975) statement that facial expressions of basic emotions are universal. How has recent research called their statement into question? [41-42]

4. How do people respond when others: a) maintain high levels of gazing; b) avoid eye contact; and c) stare at them? [42]

5. Describe how body language can communicate emotion, including examples from ballet, restaurant servers, and gestures. [42-44]

6. Describe the effects of touching, including how being touched by a waitress in the Crusco and Wetzel (1984) study affected the size of customers' tips. [44-45]

7. Compare our reaction when someone smiles while presenting information versus our reaction when someone frowns while presenting the same information. Explain the difference in terms of the cognitive tuning model. [45-47]

8. Based on Jones and Davis' theory of correspondent inference, understand the three circumstances that lead us to infer that behavior reflects underlying traits. [50]

9. Using Kelley's theory of attribution, distinguish between internal and external causes of behavior, and define the concepts of consensus, distinctiveness, and consistency. [52]

10. Compare attributions when consensus is low, distinctiveness is low, and consistency is high with attributions when consensus is high, distinctiveness is high, and consistency is high. [52-53]

11. Compare attributions about a criminal whose crime stems from controllable factors with attributions when the crime stems from uncontrollable factors. [53-54]

12. Explain the discounting that occurs when two possible supporting causes for a behavior are present, and the augmenting that occurs when both a facilitative and an inhibiting factor are present. [55-57]

13. Describe the correspondence bias, and explain why it occurs. [55-57]

14. Examine the correspondence bias in individualistic cultures compared to collectivistic cultures. [58-59]

15. Describe the actor-observer effect. [59]

16. Describe the self-serving bias, and compare the cognitive and motivational explanations for self-serving bias. [59-60]

17. Examine cultural differences in susceptibility to self-serving bias. [60-61]

18. Describe the self-defeating attributional pattern that often underlies depression. [62-63]

19. Explain how the following factors influence attributions about a rape: a) belief in a just world; b) whether the rapist is a date or a stranger; and c) whether the rater is male or female. [63]

20. How did Asch's early work in which subjects formed impressions of others based on lists of traits support his assertion that forming impressions involves more than simply adding together individual traits? [65-66]

21. Understand the four factors that determine how much weight a piece of information will receive in forming an impression according to the weighted average model. [66]

22. Describe the role played by exemplars and abstractions when we make judgments about others. [66-67]

23. List self-enhancement tactics and other-enhancement tactics used in impression management, and describe research results on whether these tactics "pay off" for persons using them. [68-70]

24. To what degree are people able to control the first impressions they make on other people? [70-71]

25. Provide evidence to support the idea that we are quite accurate in social perception. [71-72]

26. Describe possible ways through which our observable physical characteristics may come to be linked to our psychological traits. [72-73]

There's More Than First Meets Your Eyes: Understanding Figures in Your Text

Turn to the figures in your text that are mentioned below and follow the discussion about how the figures can increase you understanding of research and theory.

1. Figure 2.7 (page 47) shows how we use a speaker's facial expressions as clues to tell us whether the message is threatening to us or not. If the speaker is smiling, we feel we don't have to pay too close attention. And if we're not paying close attention, we won't be influenced much by the specifics of the message (i.e., by "issues"). Instead we'll simply be influenced by generalities (i.e., by "ideology"). But when the speaker is frowning, now we're motivated to listen carefully. If we're listening carefully, we'll be influenced by the specifics more than generalities. (Figure 2.7 assumes that the listener is not otherwise motivated to pay close attention to the message; therefore motivation here requires a frowning speaker.)

2. Figure 2.11 (page 53) is central to an understanding of Kelley's important theory of causal attribution. Make sure that you understand what consensus, consistency, and distinctiveness are, and understand the pattern of information that produces an external attribution as well as the pattern that produces an internal attribution.

3. Kelley's original theory of causal attribution said that the important attributional decision made by an observer was whether the behavior is under internal or external control. Figure 2.12 (page 55) adds a new attributional dimension to the observer's judgment. The new question the observer

asks himself is whether the behavior could have been controlled by the person doing it. Regardless of whether the act was seen to be under internal or external control, quite different judgments were made about a criminal whose crime stemmed from controllable factors compared to uncontrollable factors.

4. Figure 2.13 (page 56) contrasts situations where only one possible cause can seemingly account for behavior with situations where multiple possible causal factors are present. In the top half of the figure, discounting is discussed. When only one possible cause is present, we're sure it's the cause. But if many causes could account for the behavior, we're no longer sure which causes are important. In the bottom half of the figure, augmenting is discussed. Again, when only one possible cause is present, we're relatively sure it's the cause. But if the same cause is present in the context of other factors that would have kept the person from doing what they did, now we're particularly sure that the cause (the single "facilitative" cause) is what caused the behavior to occur.

KEY TERMS: CONCEPTS YOU NEED TO UNDERSTAND

Write out the meaning of the following terms in your own words. Cover the right-hand portion of the exercise until you have finished, then check on the accuracy of your answers by comparing them with the definitions provided.

1.	nonverbal communication	information communicated via facial expressions, eye contact, body movements, posture, and, touching [40]
2.	attribution	the process by which we seek to understand others by observing their behavior and drawing conclusions about their traits [49]
3.	correspondent inference theory	Jones and Davis' theory specifying two conditions under which we infer the existence of traits in others [50]
4.	discounting principle	the tendency to attach less importance to a particular cause of behavior when other potential causes are also present [56]
5.	correspondence bias	refers to our tendency to overuse trait attributions when describing the behavior of other people [57]
6.	actor-observer effect	the tendency to attribute our own behavior to situational factors, and the behavior of others to their traits [59]
7.	self-serving bias	our tendency to view our own traits as the cause of our positive outcomes, and situational factors as the cause of our negative outcomes [59]
8.	impression management	efforts to regulate the first impressions we make in order to appear in the best light possible [68]

MATCHING:

Match each concept on the left side of the next page with an identifying phrase, word or sentence on the right side of the page. The answers may be found after the WHAT'S WRONG HERE? section.

A.	consensus is high	__ 1.	often interpreted as aggressive act
B.	other-enhancement	__ 2.	"the whole is more than the sum of the parts"
C.	slimy behavior	__ 3.	impression-management tactic
D.	primacy effect	__ 4.	produces attribution to external causes
E.	staring	__ 5.	also called fundamental attribution error
F.	Gestalt psychologists	__ 6.	warm and cold
G.	correspondence bias	__ 7.	play up to superiors, treat subordinates with disdain
H.	central traits	__ 8.	first information counts most

WHAT'S WRONG HERE?

For each statement below indicate what needs to be changed in order to make the statement correct. You will find the answers at the end of the exercise, along with pages in the text where you can find more information.

1. When other people stare at us, we generally interpret it as a sign that they like us.

2. Rounded posture in classical ballet communicates threat, whereas angular postures communicate warmth and sympathy.

3. With regard to touching, researchers have found it produces universally positive reactions.

4. When someone is smiling we are especially likely to pay careful attention to what he is saying.

5. Ottati, et al. (1997) found that participants exposed to an angry-faced speaker were more influenced by the speaker's ideology than by the issues presented.

6. The cognitive tuning model says that we can "tune out" our affect and respond solely to a speaker's message.

7. According to correspondent inference theory, we acquire especially useful information about others from behavior that they had no choice about.

8. According to correspondent inference theory, we acquire especially useful information about others when the actions they perform are high in social desirability.

9. When my attribution is influenced by the extent to which other persons react in the same manner as my target person to a particular stimulus, my attribution is being affected by the distinctiveness factor.

10. When I consider the extent to which the person I'm trying to understand reacts in the same way to this stimulus on other occasions, I am basing my attribution on the distinctiveness factor.

11. There is no difference between cultures in the degree to which correspondence bias is shown.

12. Both actors and observers generally focus on behaviors that are intentional and observable for making attributions.

13. The self-serving bias is found just as strongly among Chinese Americans as among Americans of European descent.

14. Someone who shows only dislikable behaviors is viewed more negatively than someone who directs likable behaviors toward superiors but dislikable behaviors toward subordinates.

15. We are able to consciously control all aspects of the impressions we make on others.

MATCHING ANSWERS:

1-E [42]; 2-F [65]; 3-B [68]; 4-A [52-53]; 5-G [57]; 6-H [65]; 7-C [70]; 8-D [66]

WHAT'S WRONG HERE? ANSWERS:

1. Staring usually produces unpleasant feelings and is a sign of hostility. [42]
2. Rounded postures communicate warmth; angular postures communicate threat. [43]
3. While touching often produces positive outcomes, there are many circumstances where it is inappropriate and can provoke powerful negative reactions. [45]
4. A smile is interpreted as a signal that we need not pay careful attention. [46]
5. An angry face elicited attention and careful processing of the speaker's message. [46-47]
6. Smiles tell us we need not attend carefully, whereas frowns tell us we must attend carefully. [46]
7. When behavior is freely chosen, it tells us much about the person. [50]
8. Actions high in social desirability don't tell us much about the person because these are actions most people would perform. [51]
9. This is a description of the consensus factor. [52]
10. This is a description of the consistency factor. [52]
11. The correspondence bias is greater in individualistic cultures. [58]
12. With our own behavior, we tend to focus on understanding our unintentional actions. [59]
13. The self-serving bias is stronger among Americans of European descent. [60-61]
14. Likable behaviors toward superiors but dislikable behaviors toward subordinates ("slimy behavior") is viewed especially negatively. [70]
15. Some aspects of first impressions can't be controlled, such as physical appearance and certain aspects of speech. [71]

TRUE–FALSE:

Indicate whether each of the following statements is true or false. If false, indicate why. Correct answers are found at the end of the exercise.

1. The number of emotions represented by their own distinct facial expressions is six, with contempt representing a possible seventh basic emotion.

2. The fact that only six or seven emotions are represented by distinct facial expressions means we display only six or seven different facial expressions.

3. People in different parts of the world express basic emotions quite differently from people in other parts of the world.

4. Contextual cues often modify the way we interpret a facial expression.

5. Gestures generally have the same meaning from one culture to the next.

6. Waiters who squatted down next to customers when taking drink orders received smaller tips than waiters who remained standing.

7. Waitresses who touched customers briefly when giving them their change got bigger tips.

8. We are likely to make a correspondent inference on the basis of behaviors that produce noncommon effects.

9. We are likely to attribute another person's behavior to external causes when consensus is high, consistency is high, and distinctiveness is high.

10. When someone commits a crime stemming from controllable factors, we recommend punishment focused on rehabilitation.

11. When many potential causes for a particular behavior are present, we tend to discount the importance of each cause.

12. Persons who are depressed tend to use the self–serving bias more than nondepressed persons.

13. Persons who hold a strong belief in a just world are not likely to attribute responsibility for a rape to the victim of the rape.

14. People tend to blame rape victims more when they are raped by a stranger than when they are raped by a date.

15. At first, our impressions of others consist mainly of concrete behavioral exemplars, but after we have considerable experience with the person, our impressions are based mainly on mental abstractions.

16. Flattery is not likely to succeed as an impression management tactic.

17. The text concludes that there is no link whatsoever between physical characteristics and psychological traits.

TRUE–FALSE ANSWERS:

1. True. [40]
2. False; while there are six or seven distinct facial expressions, we can express additional emotions because the six basic expressions occur in combinations and vary in intensity. [40-41]
3. False; people around the world show the same basic facial expressions. [41-42]
4. True. [41]
5. False; gestures often have meanings that are quite different across cultures. [44]
6. False; waiters who squatted down got bigger tips. [43-44]
7. True. [46]
8. True. [50]
9. True. [52-53]
10. False; controllable factors lead to punishment designed to make the criminal suffer. [54-55]
11. True. [56]
12. False; depressives tend to use the self–defeating pattern of attributions. [62]
13. False; persons who endorse just world thinking are especially likely to blame victims. [63]
14. False; more blame is attributed to a victim of date rape. [63]
15. True. [67]
16. False; this tactic, and several others, are surprisingly successful. [68-69]
17. False; there is some relationship and this may partly explain our accuracy in social perception. [72-73]

FILL IN THE BLANKS: A GUIDED REVIEW

Mentally fill in each of the blanks in the following section while covering the answers in the margin. Check each answer against the answer in the margin by uncovering as you go along.

1. Facial expressions, eye contact, body movements, posture, and touching are the basic channels for _____.

   nonverbal communication [40]

2. Generally, we interpret a high level of eye contact from another person as a sign of _____.

   liking [42]

3. When another person gazes at us in a continuous manner and maintains such contact regardless of actions on our part, the person is _____.

   staring [42]

4. Body movements that carry a specific meaning in a given culture are called _____.

   emblems [44]

5. A person who is trying to understand the causes behind someone's behavior is engaged in the process of _____.

attribution [49]

6. The theory which states that we attribute stable traits to others when their actions are freely chosen, yield distinctive, noncommon effects, and are low in social desirability is _____.

the theory of correspondent inference [50]

7. According to Kelley's theory, the basic task we face in making a causal attribution is determining whether a behavior is caused by _____ or _____ causes.

internal; external [52-53]

8. Kelley's theory of attribution says three central factors determine whether an internal of external attribution is made. These factors are _____, _____, and _____.

consensus, consistency, distinctiveness [52-53]

9. "The extent to which others react to some stimulus or event in the same manner as the person I am considering." This defines the attributional dimension of _____.

consensus [52]

10. "The extent to which the person I am considering reacts to the stimulus or event in the same way on other occasions." This defines the attributional dimension of _____.

consistency [52]

11. "The extent to which the person I am considering reacts in the same way when I change the stimulus or event to which he's reacting." This defines the attributional dimension of _____.

distinctiveness [52]

12. The notion that the importance of any potential cause of another person's behavior is reduced to the extent that other potential causes also exist is known as the _____ principle.

discounting [55-56]

13. The tendency to attach greater importance to a potential cause of behavior if the behavior occurs despite the presence of inhibitory causes in the situation is known as _____.

augmenting [55-56]

14. Our tendency to overestimate the role of dispositions in causing the behavior of others is called the _____.

correspondence bias [57]

15. We tend to see our own behavior as stemming largely from _____; we tend to see the behavior of others as stemming from _____. This type of attributional bias is known as the _____.

situational factors; internal traits; actor-observer effect. [59]

16. The tendency to attribute our own positive outcomes to internal causes and our own negative outcomes to external causes is called _____ bias.

self-serving [59]

17. The self-defeating attributional pattern shown by depressed individuals involves attributing success to _____ causes and failure to _____ causes.

external; internal [62]

18. People who believe strongly that the world is a fair place hold a view that has been called _____ .

belief in a just world [63]

19. The fact that persons described as "warm" are perceived quite differently than those described as "cold," illustrates the impact of _____ on overall impressions.

central traits [65]

20. The fact that the first traits on a list of traits influence overall impressions more than later traits is called the _____ .

primacy effect [65-66]

21. Efforts to present ourselves in ways that produce favorable first impressions are referred to as _____ .

impression management [68]

22. Impression management tactics whose purpose is to make us look good to other people are called _____ tactics.

self-enhancement [68]

23. Impression management tactics whose purpose is to make the person we're trying to impress feel good in our presence are called _____ .

other-enhancement [68-69]

MULTIPLE-CHOICE QUESTIONS: A PERSONAL QUIZ

After you have finished reading the chapter and done the other exercises in the STUDY GUIDE, take the quiz found below to test your knowledge. Indicate your answers by circling the letter of the chosen alternative. Check your answers against the answers provided at the end of the exercise.

1. How many basic emotions are represented by their own distinct facial expressions?
   a. none
   b. only one
   c. six or seven
   d. the number is limitless

2. A high level of eye contact is usually interpreted as a sign of _____, avoiding eye contact as a sign of _____, and staring as a sign of _____.
   a. friendliness; unfriendliness; hostility
   b. unfriendliness; friendliness; hostility
   c. friendliness; hostility; unfriendliness
   d. hostility; friendliness; unfriendliness

3. Aronoff, Woike, and Hyman (1992) studied body postures displayed in classical ballet and found that threatening postures were _____, while warm postures were _____.
   a. ambiguous; more easily defined
   b. easy to display; ambiguous
   c. rounded; angular
   d. angular; rounded

4. Lynn and Mynier (1993) found that in busy restaurants, the largest tips were received by
   a. female servers who remained standing while taking orders.
   b. male servers who remained standing while taking orders.
   c. female servers who squatted down next to customers while taking orders.
   d. male servers who squatted down next to customers while taking orders.

5. The cognitive tuning model suggests that a person listening to a speaker will be more influenced by the speaker's statements rather than his ideology if:
   a. the speaker displays a happy face.
   b. the speaker displays an angry face.
   c. the speaker's face is not seen.
   d. the listener engages in heuristic processing.

6. Which of the following is concerned with how we use others' behavior as a basis for inferring their stable dispositions?
   a. the cognitive tuning model
   b. correspondence bias
   c. correspondent inference theory
   d. self-presentation research

7. Assume your friend is marrying someone who has a single positive trait (very rich!), but several negative traits. Apparently your friend is marrying this person for the money. This is an example of how _____ influence(s) our attributions.
   a. noncommon effects
   b. high social desirability
   c. low social desirability
   d. noncorrespondent inferences

8. We are likely to infer that someone's behavior reflects their actual characteristics when their behavior was
   a. high in social desirability and was freely chosen.
   b. low in social desirability and was freely chosen.
   c. high in social desirability and occurred without choice.
   d. low in social desirability and occurred without choice.

9. The finding that the order of presentation of trait words influences the rating made of the person is referred to as
   a. central traits
   b. a primacy effect
   c. a correspondent inference
   d. self-enhancement

10. We are likely to attribute another person's behavior to internal causes when consensus is _____, consistency is _____, and distinctiveness is _____.
    a. high; high; high
    b. low; low; low
    c. low; high; low
    d. high; low; high

11. We are likely to attribute another person's behavior to external causes when consensus is _____, consistency is _____, and distinctiveness is _____.
    a. high; high; high
    b. low; low; low
    c. low; high; low
    d. high; low; high

12. You are less likely to think a mother is mean-tempered if you learn she was shouting at her son because he just ran out in front of traffic. This illustrates
    a. the augmenting principle.
    b. the discounting principle.
    c. the fundamental attribution error.
    d. self-serving bias.

13. If a woman was promoted in an organization that is against affirmative action, she will probably be rated
    a. especially qualified, due to discounting.
    b. especially qualified, due to augmenting.
    c. poorly qualified, due to discounting.
    d. poorly qualified, due to augmenting.

14. The correspondence bias refers to our tendency to
    a. explain others' actions in terms of traits.
    b. explain others' actions in terms of situations.
    c. give ourselves more credit for our own successes than we really deserve.
    d. overestimate the role of situations in causing our own behavior.

15. Dispositional causes are easier to notice than situational causes. This explains the
    a. self-serving bias.
    b. depressive attribution style.
    c. primacy effect.
    d. correspondence bias.

16. The actor-observer difference suggests we perceive that our own behavior stems largely from _____, whereas we perceive the behavior of other persons stems largely from _____.
    a. situational causes; internal causes
    b. internal causes; situational causes
    c. dispositional causes; internal causes
    d. external causes; situational causes

17. Self–serving bias refers to our tendency to
    a. use situational attributions for our own behavior.
    b. use internal attributions for our own behavior.
    c. use internal attributions for our good outcomes, and external attributions for our bad outcomes.
    d. use internal attributions for our bad outcomes, and external attributions for our good outcomes.

18. Attributions blaming the victim in a rape are most strongly made when
    a. a male is rating a case of date rape.
    b. a female is rating a case of date rape.
    c. a male is rating a case of stranger rape.
    d. a female is rating a case of stranger rape.

19. When the first information presented about a person carries the most weight in the final impression formed of the person, we have an example of the
    a. fundamental attribution error.
    b. false consensus effect.
    c. base-rate fallacy.
    d. primacy effect.

20. All of the following are examples of self-enhancement techniques of impression management except
    a. wearing perfume.
    b. dressing in particular clothes.
    c. developing a suntan to improve personal appearance.
    d. directing flattering remarks to your target.

MULTIPLE–CHOICE ANSWERS

1. c [40]	6. c [50]	11. a [52-53]	16. a [59]
2. a [42]	7. a [50]	12. b [55-56]	17. c [59]
3. d [43]	8. b [50-51]	13. b [55-56]	18. a [63]
4. d [43-44]	9. b [65-66]	14. a [57]	19. d [66]
5. b [46-47]	10. c [53-54]	15. d [58]	20. d [68-69]

IF YOU'D LIKE TO KNOW MORE: FURTHER SOURCES OF INFORMATION

Goleman, D. (1982, August). Can You Tell When Someone is Lying to You? PSYCHOLOGY TODAY, 14–23. An interesting and valuable interpersonal skill!

Brandt, A. (1980, December). Face Reading: The Persistence of Physiognomy. PSYCHOLOGY TODAY, 90–96. How much can we tell about a person from his/her face or other features?

Rosenthal, Robert, et al. (1974, September). Body Talk and Tone of Voice: The Language Without Words. PSYCHOLOGY TODAY, 64-71. A visual test is discussed that measures sensitivity to nonverbal messages. Women are better at analyzing nonverbal messages than men.

Greene, David and Lepper, Mark R. (1974, September). Intrinsic Motivation: How to Turn Play into Work. PSYCHOLOGY TODAY, 49-52. A brief introduction to Greene and Lepper's well-known work on how rewards can undermine intrinsic motivation.

Beier, Ernst G. (1974, October). Nonverbal Communication: How we Send Emotional Messages. PSYCHOLOGY TODAY, 52. Our faces, our intonations, the ways we hold our bodies often send emotional messages we don't intend.

Go to http://depts.washington.edu/iat/measure2.html. The Implicit Association test asks you to make judgments about people based on their names. It points out that names provide hints as to people's sex, ethnicity, and age. Are you influenced by these dimensions?

Go to http://zzyx.ucsc.edu/~archer/. Are you interested in nonverbal communication? This page introduces the topic and gives you a chance to see if you can "read" nonverbal communications by looking at sample pictures and trying to guess what each picture shows.

Go to http://psych-server.iastate.edu/facutly/gwells/   This is the home page of Gary Wells, a professor of psychology at Iowa State University and a nationally recognized expert on eyewitness identification processes. If you scroll down, you'll find some interesting demonstrations to find out how good you are at recognizing criminal suspects captured on security videos. (Wells' work is discussed in a later chapter of your text.)

Go to http://mambo.ucsc.edu/psl/fanl.html. This site provides many interesting pictures of faces and challenges us to think about how we go about determining underlying emotions on the basis of facial expressions.

THINKING CRITICALLY ABOUT SOCIAL PERCEPTION

1. Self-serving bias refers to our tendency to attribute our personal successes to internal causes, but to attribute our personal failures to external causes. An important attributional task for college students is to understand performance on exams. Consider your best recent exam performance. What caused you to do so well? Now consider a recent exam where your performance was disappointing. Why didn't you do so well? When you compare your attributions for good performance and your attributions for poorer performance, can you find elements of self-serving bias? (An obvious example of self-servingness would be to explain your good performance in terms of studying hard and knowing the material, while explaining your poor performance by saying the test was hard.)

2. Look for applications of attribution theory in advertising. Try to find   advertisements that present consensus, distinctiveness, or consistency information in such a way that we are led to attribute positive qualities to the product. Or you might be able to find applications of the discounting and

augmenting principles. Would an advertising specialist benefit from knowing the rules of attribution?

3. Imagine yourself interviewing for a job that you consider to be the "ideal job" for you. In other words, you want to do everything in your power to maximize you chances of being hired for this job! Based on social psychological research on social perception, what could you do to enhance the first impression you make on the interviewer? Should you worry about your nonverbal communication? Should you deliberately try to manage the impression you're making? Should you worry about appearing deceitful by accidentally projecting cues that indicate lying?

4. Do we form impressions of people based on their names? Imagine a person named Michael or Matt. List five characteristics that come to mind for this person. Next imagine a person named Sheldon or Winthrop. Again, list five characteristics. Do your two lists differ? Another way to consider this question is to think of friends who have unusual names and others who have "popular" names. Do any of these persons feel that their first names cause others to respond to them in a stereotypic manner?

5. An interesting question revolves around the characteristics that are attractive to members of the opposite sex. With regard to what characteristics women find attractive in men, for instance, common knowledge provides us with conflicting answers. Sometimes it is suggested that women like nice guys, but a common expression has it that nice guys finish last. Is there truth in either of these notions?

3 SOCIAL COGNITION: THINKING ABOUT THE SOCIAL WORLD

CHAPTER OUTLINE: GETTING THE OVERALL PICTURE:

Before reading the chapter, it may be helpful to examine the chapter outline. This will give you an idea of what is covered in the chapter and should help you organize your learning and review the material. You can also record notes on text sections under the outline headings for those sections.

I. Schemas: Mental Frameworks for Organizing—and Using—Social Information

    A. Types of Schemas: Persons, Roles, and Events

    B. The Impact of Schemas on Social Cognition: Attention, Encoding, Retrieval

    C. Cornerstones of Social Psychology: Evidence for the Self-Confirming Nature of Schemas: When—and Why—Beliefs Shape Reality

II. Heuristics: Mental Shortcuts in Social Cognition

    A. Representativeness: Judging by Resemblance

    B. Availability: "If I Can Think of It, It Must Be Important"

        1. Priming: Some Effects of Increased Availability

III. Potential Sources of Error in Social Cognition: Why Total Rationality Is Scarcer Than You Think

    A. Rational versus Intuitive Processing: Going with Our Gut-Level Feelings Even When We Know Better

    B. Beyond the Headlines: As Social Psychologists See It—Do Safety Devices Save Lives? Don't Bet On It!

    C. Dealing with Inconsistent Information: Paying Attention to What Doesn't Fit

    D. The Optimistic Bias for Task Completion: Why We Often Think We Can Do More, Sooner, Than We Really Can

E. The Potential Costs of Thinking Too Much: Why, Sometimes, Our Tendency to Do As Little Cognitive Work As Possible May Be Justified

F. Counterfactual Thinking: The Effects of Considering "What Might Have Been"

G. Magical Thinking: Would You Eat a Chocolate Shaped Like a Spider?

H. Thought Suppression: Why Efforts to Avoid Thinking Certain Thoughts Sometimes Backfire

I. Social Cognition: A Word of Optimism

IV. Affect and Cognition: How Feelings Shape Thought and Thought Shapes Feelings

A. Connections between Affect and Cognition: Some Intriguing Effects

1. The Influence of Affect on Cognition

2. The Influence of Cognition on Affect

B. The Affect Infusion Model: How Affect Influences Cognition

C. Social Diversity: A Critical Analysis—Culture and the Appraisal of Emotions

LEARNING OBJECTIVES: WHAT YOU SHOULD LEARN

As you are reading the chapter, these objectives provide page–by–page questions for you to answer. Answering the objectives should assure that you understand the essential material in the chapter.

1. Define the concept of schema, and give an example illustrating person schemas, role schemas, and event schemas. [81-83]

2. Examine how schemas influence attention, encoding, and retrieval of information. [83-84]

3. How did Rosenthal and Jacobson show that schemas held by teachers can produce self-fulfilling effects in a classroom? [84-85]

4. Describe the basic nature of heuristics, indicating how they allow us to remain reasonably accurate while reducing cognitive effort and avoiding information overload. [86]

5. Describe the representativeness heuristic, and indicate how use of this heuristic sometimes leads us to commit the base-rate fallacy. [86]

6. Summarize how our judgments regarding others are affected by the availability heuristic, and indicate when we follow the "amount of information" rule and when we follow the "ease of recall" rule. [86-88]

7. Give an example that illustrates how priming influences social cognition. [88-89]

8. Compare rational and intuitive thinking, and explain why we often rely on intuitive thinking. [90-91]

9. Why is there a tendency to overestimate the advantages of airbags and antilock brakes? [91-92]

10. Examine the circumstances under which unexpected "inconsistent" information grabs our attention and influences later social judgments. [93-94]

11. Summarize research on the planning fallacy, noting subjects' thinking mode during planning, their attributions concerning past failures, and the role of task motivation. [94-96]

12. Based on the Wilson and Schooler (1991) study, indicate how "thinking too much" while rating jams (or making other ratings) lowered the accuracy of participants' ratings. [96-97]

13. Consider the effects of counterfactual thinking in each of the following cases: a) you imagine a worse outcome than you actually received; b) you imagine a better outcome than you actually received; c) you think about the major regrets of your life; and d) you plan strategies to improve future performance. [97-100]

14. Describe various forms of magical thinking, including the law of contagion, the law of similarity, and the reactions to missile attacks by Gulf War residents. [100-101]

15. Describe the process by which thoughts are suppressed, and describe the rebound effect that occurs when individuals lack sufficient resources to successfully suppress. [101-103]

16. What happens when people high in reactance are instructed to suppress their most frequently occurring intrusive thought? [103-104]

17. What is the text's conclusion with regard to our ability to overcome the limitations inherent in social cognition? [104]

18. Describe how our current mood influences how our response to new stimuli and the style of information processing we adopt. [105-106]

19. Describe how our current mood influences memory through mood dependent memory and mood congruence effects. [106]

20. Describe how our current mood influences creativity and negotiators' strategies and expectations. [106-107]

21. What happened when jurors were instructed to ignore emotion-provoking information in the Edwards and Bryan (1997) study? [107-108]

22. Describe the three ways in which our cognition can influence our current emotions. [108-109]

23. Using Forgas' (1994) Affect Infusion Model, explain the two mechanisms through which feelings influence social thought. [109]

24. Understand the prediction derived from the Affect Infusion Model stating that affective states are more likely to influence social judgment when we engage in careful thought than when we engage in more automatic thinking. [109-110]

25. Examine similarities and differences in the appraisal of emotions across cultures. [111-112]

There's More Than First Meets Your Eyes: Understanding Figures in Your Text

Turn to the figures in your text that are mentioned below and follow the discussion about how the figures can increase you understanding of research and theory.

1. Figure 3.4 (page 88) shows a study where subjects were given different instructions regarding how to go about thinking of examples of rude behavior by members of their own gender ("ingroup") or by the other gender ("outgroup"). Some subjects were to think of three examples, while other subjects were to think of six examples. It's assumed that subjects can think of three examples of rudeness quickly, and the speed rule says if you can think of examples quickly, the person is rude. When subjects are asked to think of six examples, that's a lot of information, but if you can do it, the quantity rule says the person is rude. Which rule is stronger? When judging outgroups, speed is more important. When judging ingroups, quantity is more important.

2. The planning fallacy refers to our tendency to think we can finish a task in less time than it actually takes. Figure 3.8 (page 95) suggests that we are especially prone to thinking we can get something done early if we are strongly motivated to get it done. Filing my taxes when I expect a refund? I expect I'll get it done very early! Filing my taxes when I'm not expecting a refund? I expect it will take longer. In fact both groups take about as long to get their return filed.

3. Figure 3.11 (page 104) describes the effects created when subjects were instructed to avoid certain thoughts (i.e., to "suppress"). Basically, subjects were successful in suppressing thoughts except for subjects with the personality characteristic called high reactance. Persons high in reactance respond to a direct request as if it were a threat to their freedom, and in this study, the request to suppress apparently threatened high reactance subjects. To reassert their freedom these subjects did not go along with the request.

4. Figure 3.14 (page 108) suggests that jurors are not able to suppress certain thoughts just because they are instructed to do so. In fact, not only were these jurors unable to suppress, they were actually greatly influenced by the very thoughts they were told to suppress. This happened mainly when the thoughts they were supposed to suppress were emotion-provoking.

5. Figure 3.15 (page 110) presents the affect infusion model. The basic assumption of this model is that we are influenced by how we feel (our "affect") while making social judgments. When we jump to straightforward decisions, the judgment is so automatic that we're not influenced by affect. But when we think more effortfully, affect often influences our decisions. In the text two mechanisms are described that lead the person thinking effortfully to be more influenced by affect.

KEY TERMS: CONCEPTS YOU NEED TO UNDERSTAND

Write out the meaning of the following terms in your own words. Cover the right–hand portion of the exercise until you have finished, then check on the accuracy of your answers by comparing them with the definitions provided.

1. schema — mental frameworks regarding some aspect of our social world that helps us to organize and interpret social information [81-83]

2. representativeness heuristic — a mental short–cut in which we decide whether an individual belongs to a particular group based on whether the individual resembles "typical" members of the group [86]

3. availability heuristic — the notion that if we can quickly remember information or remember quite a bit, it must be important; we use this as a mental short–cut in making social inferences [86-88]

4. priming — any event that heightens the availability of some category of information so that this category is now readily accessed in some unrelated context [88-89]

5. counterfactual thinking — our tendency to evaluate events by thinking about "what might have been." The more easily alternative possibilities come to mind, the stronger our reaction to events that actually occurred [97]

6. affect infusion model — says that how we feel influences our thinking in two ways: mood primes related cognitions and mood acts as a heuristic cue [109-110]

MATCHING:

Match each concept on the left with an identifying phrase, word or sentence on the right. The answers follow the WHAT'S WRONG HERE? section.

A.	law of contagion	—	1.	optimistic bias for task completion
B.	planning fallacy	—	2.	caused by priming
C.	person high in reactance	—	3.	suppressed thoughts increase in frequency
D.	medical student syndrome	—	4.	believing something is true causes us to make it happen
E.	self-fulfilling prophecy	—	5.	example of magical thinking
F.	heuristic	—	6.	reacts negatively when perceives a threat to personal freedom
G.	rebound effect	—	7.	event schema
H.	script	—	8.	short-cut rule for making decisions

WHAT'S WRONG HERE?

For each statement below indicate what needs to be changed in order to make the statement correct. You will find the answers at the end of the exercise, along with pages in the text where you can find more information.

1. We generally pay greater attention to consistent information than to information inconsistent with an existing schema.

2. Because of the fact that information inconsistent with our schemas is readily noticed, it is guaranteed that this information will influence later social thought.

3. Words that start with "k" are more common than words that have "k" as their third letter.

4. When you expect a performer to do well, good performance gets your attention more readily than an unexpected poor performance.

5. Inconsistent information grabs our attention, and thus truly bizarre information has considerable long-term impact on us.

6. If a person considers past experiences in which tasks took longer than expected, the planning fallacy will disappear.

7. Raters who carefully analyzed the reasons for their ratings of various strawberry jams more closely matched the ratings of experts than raters who simply rated the jams.

8. We feel more sympathy for a woman robbed by a hitchhiker she picked up if she frequently picked up hitchhikers in the past.

9. People are not likely to engage in magical thinking when they are under stress.

MATCHING ANSWERS:

1–B [94]   4–E [85]   7–H [82]
2–D [88]   5–A [101]   8–F [86]
3–G [103]   6–C [103-104]

WHAT'S WRONG HERE? ANSWERS:

1. Inconsistent information grabs our attention. [93]
2. Noticed information <u>is</u> more likely to enter memory, but sometimes we notice and then discount inconsistent information. [93-94]
3. Most people estimate that words starting with "k" are more common, but they are victims of the availability heuristic. [86-87]
4. When a performer violates our expectations we're especially likely to notice the level of performance. [88]
5. Truly bizarre information is attention-grabbing, but we tend to discount the information after noticing it. [93-94]
6. Rather than becoming a more rational planner, the person tends to explain away the earlier experience. [94]
7. Introspecting on the reasons for one's ratings makes the rater less accurate. [96-97]
8. We feel sympathy for the woman who seldom picked up hitchhikers because we can imagine an alternative action. [97-98]
9. High stress <u>does</u> increase magical thinking, but people <u>low</u> in tolerance for ambiguity are more susceptible to this style of thinking. [101]

TRUE–FALSE:

Indicate whether each of the following statements is true or false. If false, indicate why. Correct answers are found at the end of the exercise.

1. Automatic priming refers to priming that occurs even though the person is not aware of the priming stimuli.

2. A rational thinker realizes that there is just as good a chance of drawing a red jelly bean from a jar where 1 or 10 beans are red as from a jar where 10 of 100 beans are red.

3. The text states that there is much rational data showing that air bags save lives, but that people tend to discount the information contained in this research.

4. While we readily notice schema-inconsistent information, our thinking is oftentimes not affected because we discount the schema-inconsistent information.

5. With regard to when they plan on filing their tax return, people expecting a tax refund are no more likely to commit the planning fallacy than people not expecting a refund.

6. When people are asked to identify what they regret from their entire lives, they regret what they didn't do more often than what they did.

7. A sweater, kept in a sealed plastic bag and never touched by its owner, is rated less favorably just because its owner has AIDS.

8. Persons who are high in reactance are especially likely to experience a rebound effect when attempting to suppress unwanted thoughts.

9. Persons experiencing positive affect are not very likely to show the fundamental attribution error.

10. Persons experiencing positive affect demonstrate lowered creativity.

11. When Edwards and Bryan (1997) instructed "jurors" to ignore emotion-provoking information regarding a defendant, jurors were generally able to do it.

12. Our social judgments and decisions are more likely to be influenced by affect infusion when we engage in careful, analytic thinking than when we rely on simple, automatic thinking.

13. How we appraise emotion-provoking situations is related to the degree of urbanization of our culture.

TRUE–FALSE ANSWERS:

1. True. [89]
2. True. [90]
3. False; it's argued that people intuitively believe in air bags, despite a lack of supporting data. [91-92]
4. True. [93-94]
5. False; people expecting a refund showed the planning fallacy to a greater extent. [94-95]
6. True. [98]
7. True. [100-101]
8. True. [103-104]
9. False; positive affect makes us focus on readily available information, thereby increasing this error. [106]
10. False; positive affect is associated with increased creativity. [106]
11. False; in fact, jurors told to ignore the information rated the defendant most harshly of all jurors. [107-108]
12. True. [109-110]
13. True. [111-112]

FILL IN THE BLANKS: A GUIDED REVIEW

Mentally fill in each of the blanks in the following section while covering the answers in the margin. Check each answer against the answer in the margin by uncovering as you go along.

1.   The tendency for beliefs and schemas to remain unchanged even in the face of contradictory information is called the _____ effect.   perseverance [84]

2.   When we exceed our capacity to process new information we enter a state of _____.   information overload [86]

3.   The term referring to basic decision-making principles that allow us to make social judgments quickly and easily is _____.   heuristics [86]

4.   To determine whether someone is a coach, I compare his traits to those of the "average" coach. In deciding whether he is a coach, I am using the _____ heuristic.   representativeness [86]

5.   In making a judgment about a specific event, people often fail to take into account how likely the event is generally. This describes our tendency to ignore _____.   base-rates [86]

6.   When my evaluation of someone is influenced by how quickly I can bring to mind relevant instances of the behavior I am judging, I am using the _____ heuristic.   availability [87]

7.   When exposure to specific stimuli or events causes people to use these stimuli or events to interpret subsequent events, we have an example of _____.   priming [88]

8.   I think I have a better chance of drawing a red jelly bean from a jar where 10 beans out of 100 are red than from another jar where 1 bean out of 10 is red. Apparently, I'm a victim of _____ thinking.   intuitive [90]

9.   The tendency to underestimate the time needed to complete a major project is called the _____.   planning fallacy [94]

10.   When we an easily conceive of an alternative to what actually happened, a "what might have been" response is readily evoked. The pattern of thinking that occurs is called _____.   counterfactual thinking [97]

11.   Efforts to prevent certain thoughts from entering consciousness are referred to as _____.   thought suppression [102]

12.   _____ refers to the fact that what we remember in a given mood may be determined by what we learned when previously in that mood.   mood-dependent memory [106]

13.   Our tendency to remember positive information when in a positive mood and negative information when in a negative mood is called a _____ effect.   mood congruence [106]

41

14. The full name for the AIM, which explains the mechanisms through which affect influences social thought and social judgment, is _____.

affect infusion
model [109-110]

MULTIPLE-CHOICE QUESTIONS: A PERSONAL QUIZ

After you have finished reading the chapter and done the other exercises in the STUDY GUIDE, take the quiz found below to test your knowledge. Indicate your answers by circling the letter of the chosen alternative. Check your answers against the answers provided at the end of the exercise.

1. Which is an example of the representativeness heuristic?
   a. To determine whether someone is a lawyer, I compare his traits to the "average" lawyer.
   b. To determine whether someone is "conscientious," I try to recall instances of such behavior.
   c. To determine my impressions of someone, I combine the available bits of information to find an average.
   d. To determine whether someone is "conscientious," I engage in priming.

2. In making a judgment about a specific instance, people often fail to take into account how prevalent or frequent something is in general. This describes the
   a. confirmation bias.
   b. false consensus effect.
   c. regression fallacy.
   d. base–rate fallacy.

3. When my judgment of whether someone is aggressive is determined by how many relevant instances of aggressive behavior I can recall, I am using _____ to make my judgment.
   a. the representativeness heuristic
   b. a stereotype
   c. visual imagery
   d. the availability heuristic

4. The cognitive framework that helps us to interpret what is expected to happen in a particular setting or situation is
   a. a role schema.
   b. a person schema.
   c. a self schema.
   d. an event schema.

5. When planting certain ideas or categories in people's minds causes them to use these ideas or categories to interpret subsequent events, we have an example of
   a. priming.
   b. the representativeness heuristic.
   c. confirmation bias.
   d. the fundamental attribution error.

6. The cognitive-experiential self-theory postulates two distinct modes of thinking. These two modes are:
   a. intuitive thought and deliberate, rational thought.
   b. consistent thought and inconsistent thought.
   c. biased thought and unbiased thought.
   d. affective thought and cognitive thought.

7. The planning fallacy refers to the tendency to
   a. plan more activities in one's lifetime than can possibly be completed.
   b. put off important decisions until the last possible moment.
   c. give up plans because of a seeming lack of time.
   d. be overly optimistic in predicting how long a given task will take.

8. Which individual is most likely to commit the planning fallacy when filing her tax return?
   a. Not strongly motivated and expecting a refund.
   b. Not strongly motivated and not expecting a refund.
   c. Strongly motivated and not expecting a refund.
   d. Strongly motivated and expecting a refund.

9. John received a B in his class, just barely missing an A. Art, on the other hand, just barely got a B. Which of the following is probably true?
   a. John engages in downward counterfactual thinking and is relatively satisfied.
   b. John engages in upward counterfactual thinking and is relatively dissatisfied.
   c. John engages in downward counterfactual thinking and is relatively dissatisfied.
   d. John engages in upward counterfactual thinking and is relatively satisfied.

10. A computer I've really wanted was on sale at 50% off, but I was too busy to get to the store. Now it's on sale again at 25% off. What does counterfactual thinking predict about my buying it now?
    a. I won't buy it because it will remind me of when it was 50% off.
    b. I'll buy it so I won't feel bad when it goes off sale again.
    c. Action inertia will cause me to buy it this time.
    d. None of the above; this situation is irrelevant to counterfactual thinking.

11. When students sampled and rated various strawberry jams, they were more likely to make accurate ratings of the jams when
    a. they carefully analyzed reasons why they rated each product as they did.
    b. they thought about each piece of information and how it would impact their decision.
    c. they merely rated the products.
    d. both a and b were effective, since both incorporate deep thinking.

12. The counterfactual thinking hypothesis suggests that the person who gets robbed by a hitchhiker he picked up will experience greater regret if
    a. he frequently picks up hitchhikers.
    b. he hardly ever picks up hitchhikers.
    c. he cannot imagine himself doing anything but picking up the hitchhiker.
    d. he hears a news report emphasizing the importance of avoiding hitchhikers.

13. When research participants were asked to report their single most regrettable action or inaction from their entire lives
    a. their more frequent regret was a particular thing they had done.
    b. their most frequent regret was a past failure to do something.
    c. they were just as likely to mention an action as an inaction.
    d. high self-monitors mentioned actions, while low self-monitors mentioned inactions.

14. Which type of error in social cognition is illustrated by the fact that we might feel squeamish eating a chocolate shaped like a spider?
    a. affect infusion
    b. counterfactual thinking
    c. intuitive thinking
    d. magical thinking

15. When does a rebound effect happen?
    a. after we finish appraising our emotions
    b. when we are recovering from a negative mood
    c. after we've been suppressing an unwanted thought
    d. when we're presented with information contradictory to our schema

16. Unwanted intrusive thoughts occur most often for
    a. low reactance persons allowed to express their thoughts in writing.
    b. high reactance persons allowed to express their thoughts in writing.
    c. low reactance persons instructed to suppress intrusive thoughts.
    d. high reactance persons instructed to suppress intrusive thoughts.

17. How is people's thinking affected by their current mood?
    a. Thinking and affect are not related to one another.
    b. People in a good mood tend to think happy thoughts and are also more creative.
    c. People in a good mood tend to think unhappy thoughts and are also more creative.
    d. People in a good mood are more creative but there is no impact on happy/unhappy thinking.

18. Which information had the most impact on "jurors'" ratings of a defendant in the study by Edwards and Bryan (1997)?
    a. Neutral information said to be admissible.
    b. Neutral information that was to be ignored.
    c. Emotion-provoking information said to be admissible.
    d. Emotion-provoking information that was to be ignored.

19. The affect-as-information mechanism says that affect influences cognition because our feelings act as
    a. a prime.
    b. a motivator.
    c. a counterfactual thought.
    d. a heuristic cue.

20. Under which condition is affect infusion most likely to occur when a person is thinking about a relatively unimportant topic?
    a. The person is engaged in analytic, effortful thinking triggered by the priming mechanism.
    b. The person is engaged in analytic, effortful thinking triggered by the affect-as-information mechanism.
    c. The person is engaged in simple, automatic thinking.
    d. None of the above; affect infusion doesn't happen with unimportant topics.

MULTIPLE–CHOICE ANSWERS

1. a [86]	6. a [90]	11. c [97]	16. d [103-104]
2. d [86]	7. d [94]	12. b [98]	17. b [106]
3. d [86-87]	8. d [94-95]	13. b [98]	18. d [107-108]
4. d [82]	9. b [98]	14. d [100-101]	19. d [109]
5. a [88-89]	10. a [99]	15. c [102-103]	20. a [109-110]

IF YOU'D LIKE TO KNOW MORE: FURTHER SOURCES OF INFORMATION

Langer, E. J. (1982, April). Automated Lives. PSYCHOLOGY TODAY, 60–71. Langer discusses the   tendency to engage in "mindlessness"—to do things and to make decisions without really thinking.

Gmelch, G. and Felson, R. (1980, December). Can a Lucky Charm Get You Through Organic Chemistry? PSYCHOLOGY TODAY, 75–78. A large majority of college students employ rituals and charms to try to influence the fates.

Hughes, M. and Gove, W. R. (1981, October). Playing Dumb. PSYCHOLOGY TODAY, 74–80. Feigning ignorance in situations where it is to one's benefit to do so is a form of "impression management." This report suggests that men are more likely than women to pretend to be less intelligent than they really are.

Go to http://www.psych.nwu.edu/psych/people/faculty/roese/research/cf/cfnews.htm It's called the Counterfactual Research News site and it gets you to think about how your life might have unfolded differently. What if you had studied harder in school? What if you had asked out so-and-so when you had the chance?

Go to http://www.vcu.edu/hasweb/psy/faculty/fors/psy321/h.htm   A fascinating demonstration is provided to show how cognitive rules of thumb ("heuristics") operate. You'll be amazed at the ability of this site to read your mind.

THINKING CRITICALLY ABOUT SOCIAL COGNITION

1. We have surprisingly detailed schemas regarding the characteristics possessed by many groups. For example, we have well-developed schemas for the elderly. Simply mentioning the word "grandmother" undoubtedly triggers many ideas and images for you. What occupations would you expect a grandmother to hold? What type of clothes do you expect a grandmother to wear? What kind of car does a grandmother drive? Despite the fact that we know grandmothers vary considerably from one another, it is probably the case that fairly distinct pictures come into your mind as you consider these questions.

2. A practical lesson for everyone is found in Chapter 3 in the discussion of the planning fallacy. When is the last time that you finished a major class project in less time than you anticipated? On the other hand, when is the last time a major class project took considerably longer than you anticipated? There's a good chance that you can easily think of projects that took longer than you anticipated, but have a harder time thinking of projects that took less time than you thought. It wouldn't be a bad idea to read the planning fallacy section in your textbook again the next time you face a major project!

3. There are many instances where counterfactual thinking influences our feelings. Counterfactual thinking occurs when alternative outcomes to what actually happened can readily be brought to mind. Persons who missed their plane flight and later learn that the plane crashed certainly have a dramatic experience of what might have been. Another instance of counterfactual thinking occurs in immediate reactions of competitors who win silver compared to bronze medals. A study published in the JOURNAL OF PERSONALITY AND SOCIAL PSYCHOLOGY in 1995 produced the counterintuitive finding that second place finishers in the Olympics experience more negative affect as a result of their finish than third place finishers. How can individuals in an objectively better position feel worse off than those who finish below them? The answer lies in their counterfactual thinking processes. For the second place finisher, the most salient thought is that he/she might have won. For the third place finisher, the most salient thought is that he/she might have received no medal at all. Can you think of instances where you've been influenced by counterfactual thinking?

4. Try to think of personal examples of the other biases discussed. To the degree you can come up with good personalized examples, it should improve your memory for the particular bias.

4 ATTITUDES: EVALUATING THE SOCIAL WORLD

CHAPTER OUTLINE: GETTING THE OVERALL PICTURE:

Before reading the chapter, it may be helpful to examine the chapter outline. This will give you an idea of what is covered in the chapter and should help you organize your learning and review the material. You can also record notes on text sections under the outline headings for those sections.

I. Forming Attitudes: How We Come to Hold the Views We Do

    A. Social Learning: Acquiring Attitudes from Others

        1. Classical Conditioning: Learning Based on Association

        2. Instrumental Conditioning: Learning to Hold the "Right" Views

        3. Observational Learning: Learning by Example

    B. Social Comparison and Attitude Formation

    C. Genetic Factors: Some Surprising Recent Findings

II. Do Attitudes Influence Behavior? And If So, When and How?

    A. Cornerstones of Social Psychology: Attitudes versus Actions: "When Saying Is Definitely Not Doing"

    B. When Do Attitudes Influence Behavior? Specificity, Strength, Accessibility, and Other Factors

        1. Aspects of the Situation: Factors that Prevent Us from Expressing Our Attitudes

        2. Aspects of Attitudes Themselves

            a. Attitude Origins

1. Is Dissonance Really Unpleasant?

B. Dissonance and Attitude Change: The Effects of Induced Compliance

1. Dissonance and the Less-Leads-to-More Effect

C. Dissonance as a Tool for Beneficial Changes in Behavior: When Hypocrisy Can Be a Force for Good

D. Social Diversity: A Critical Analysis—Is Dissonance Culture-Bound? Evidence from a Cross-National Study

LEARNING OBJECTIVES: WHAT YOU SHOULD LEARN

As you are reading the chapter, these objectives provide page–by–page questions for you to answer. Answering the objectives should assure that you understand the essential material in the chapter.

1. Examine the textbook's definition of "attitude" and note reasons why attitudes are important. [118-119]

2. Describe evidence to support the idea that attitudes can be formed via classical conditioning, including subliminal conditioning. [121-122]

3. Explain how attitudes can be strengthened or weakened through instrumental conditioning. [122]

4. Explain how attitudes are acquired via observational learning. [122-123]

5. Explain how the social comparison process influences the formation of attitudes. [123]

6. Compare attitude similarity between identical and nonidentical twins. Which attitudes show heritability? Explain how inherited general dispositions may be the underlying basis for genetic influences on attitudes. [124-125]

7. Describe the attitude-behavior inconsistency observed in the LaPiere (1934) study. [126-127]

8. How do the following aspects of the situation often prevent us from expressing our attitudes?
   a) situational constraints; b) the fact that we choose attitude-supporting situations. [127-128]

9. How are these aspects of attitudes related to whether people will act on their attitudes? a) attitude origins; b) attitude strength; c) attitude importance; d) vested interest; and e) attitude specificity. [128-130]

10. Based on the theory of reasoned action, describe the three factors that determine whether a person with the opportunity to engage in careful thought will develop a behavioral intention to perform a particular action. [131]

11. What factors attitudes influence our behavior when we must act quickly and spontaneously? (Answer from the point of view of the attitude-to-behavior-process model an the prototype/willingness model.) [131-133]

12. Which attitudes predict students' use of sunscreen and which attitudes fail to predict? Explain these findings in terms of attitude-behavior consistency models. [131-134]

13. Summarize the early approach to persuasion, and know the six classic research findings reviewed by the textbook. [135-136]

14. Understand the differences between the central and peripheral routes to persuasion, and describe circumstances under which we engage in each of these modes of thought. [136]

15. Describe how our tendency to engage in effortful, systematic processing of persuasive messages is influenced by accuracy motivation, defensive motivation, and impression motivation. [137-138]

16. Examine the idea that attitudes can serve different functions for the person holding them. [138-139]

17. When is a speaker who speaks in a nervous and unfriendly manner especially unlikely to persuade us? Under what circumstances is the speaker's style relatively unimportant? [139-140]

18. Understand how reactance explains the fact that we often show negative attitude change when faced with hard-sell persuasion attempts. [140-141]

19. Describe why we are better able to resist persuasive messages when they are preceded by forewarning of persuasive intent. [141]

20. Describe how selective avoidance and selective exposure help us resist persuasion. [141]

21. Describe research demonstrating how biased assimilation and attitude polarization help us resist persuasion. [141-143]

22. Define cognitive dissonance, and describe three direct tactics and four indirect tactics people can use to get rid of dissonance. [144-145]

23. How did researchers document the view that dissonance is physiologically arousing <u>and</u> unpleasant? How did they show that the discomfort of dissonance often motivates attitude change? [145-146]

24. Describe the attitude change that occurs following induced compliance, and indicate why (and under what circumstances) the less-leads-to-more effect occurs. [145-146]

25. Describe how the hypocrisy procedure can be used to get sexually-active subjects to no longer engage in unprotected sex. [149-151]

26. Explain why the spreading of alternatives effect occurred for Canadian students but not for Japanese students. [151-152]

There's More Than First Meets Your Eyes: Understanding Figures in Your Text

Turn to the figures in your text that are mentioned below and follow the discussion about how the figures can increase you understanding of research and theory.

1. Figure 4.3 (page 121) shows how we can acquire emotional reactions to persons and events simply by observing how other people react to these same events. This is a special case of classical conditioning, often referred to by the term "vicarious" classical conditioning. The child comes to realize that the first stimulus (member of minority group) is a "signal" for the second stimulus (an emotional reaction displayed by the parent). After a few pairings of these stimuli, the child begins to respond the same as the parent.

2. In figure 4.7 (page 130) it is demonstrated that a person's attitude about an issue will accurately predict his voting preference, particularly if the voter has a vested interest in the topic.

3. Figure 4.8 (page 132) shows that when behavior is not carefully and rationally planned, many factors other than simply the attitude must be taken into account before a researcher can predict whether the behavior will occur.

4. To understand Figure 4.12 on page 139, the reader needs to appreciate the difference between heuristic and systematic processing. The heuristic processor is not very involved in the message and changes her attitude if something about the message makes it "seem correct." If the speaker seems confident, the message must be correct. The systematic processor, on the other hand, is involved in the message and changes her attitude only if the message presents strong arguments. To the systematic processor, the speaker's style (i.e., confidence) doesn't matter.

5. Figure 4.13 (page 142) shows that people who are highly prejudiced against homosexuals find an article supporting negative stereotypes more convincing than an article refuting the same stereotypes. Similarly, persons who are not prejudiced find the article refuting the stereotypes more convincing. The general principle is that how we evaluate information depends on whether it confirms or disconfirms our existing views.

6. Figure 4.16 (page 148) assumes that an individual has engaged in attitude-discrepant behavior (usually this involves saying something that's not believed). One person does this for good, strong reasons. This person feels little sense of inconsistency and not much pressure to change his attitude. But the other person does it for weak reasons. This person feels strong inconsistency

and much pressure to change his attitude. (Note that good, strong reasons are a "large inducement" and weak reasons are a "small inducement.")

7.   Figure 4.18 (page 151) presents a study using hypocrisy to create dissonance. Hypocrisy involves having people think about times when they or others haven't done something they believe in. A person who thinks about this will feel dissonance and will have a need to reduce the dissonance. How will they reduce the dissonance? It depends on whether they think about their own failure to do something they believe or whether they think of others' failure. With my own failure, I reduce dissonance directly by purchasing condoms. After thinking about others' failure, I reduce dissonance through less direct actions.

KEY TERMS: CONCEPTS YOU NEED TO UNDERSTAND

Write out the meaning of the following terms in your own words. Cover the right-hand portion of the exercise until you have finished, then check on the accuracy of your answers by comparing them with the definitions provided.

1. attitudes	mental representations stored in memory of objects in our social world, especially our evaluations of these objects [118]
2. elaboration likelihood model	theory that there are two routes to persuasion, differing in the amount of cognitive effort or elaboration they require [136]
3. central route to persuasion	persuasion that takes place because of careful and thoughtful consideration of the issues and arguments involved [136]
4. reactance	the negative reactions we experience when our personal freedom is threatened [140]
5. cognitive dissonance	the unpleasant internal state which occurs when a person is faced with inconsistency between attitudes and behavior, or between two attitudes [144]
6. less-leads-to-more effect	the finding that the less inducement one has for engaging in attitude-discrepant behavior, the more pressure to change the attitude [148]
7. hypocrisy	feelings occurring when one publicly advocates some attitude but becomes aware of acting inconsistently with the espoused attitude [149]

MATCHING:

Match each concept on the left with an identifying phrase, word or sentence on the right. The answers are on the next page.

A. accessible attitude	__ 1. elements of persuasion include source, message, and audience
B. forewarning	__ 2. target carefully considers message content
C. early approach to persuasion	__ 3. target is on the peripheral route
D. reactance	__ 4. advance knowledge of persuader's intent
E. systematic processing	__ 5. can be readily brought to mind
F. subliminal conditioning	__ 6. often causes negative attitude change
G. induced compliance situation	__ 7. below level of conscious awareness
H. heuristic processing	__ 8. causes attitude-discrepant statements

WHAT'S WRONG HERE?

For each statement below indicate what needs to be changed in order to make the statement correct. You will find the answers at the end of the exercise, along with pages in the text where you can find more information.

1. When affect-inducing photos were presented subliminally just before pictures of a stranger, subjects' ratings of the stranger were not affected.

2. Genetic factors play just as much of a role in shaping "gut-level" preferences as they play in shaping more "cognitive" attitudes.

3. Attitudes acquired by watching someone else interact with an attitude object generally affect our actions more than attitudes based on direct experience.

4. In 1934 LaPiere found that, consistent with the openly-expressed prejudice of the 1930s, most U.S. restaurants, etc. refused service to a young Chinese couple.

5. The appropriate question for researchers who study the attitude-behavior relationship is to determine whether behavior can be predicted from attitudes.

6. Attitudes are good at predicting behavior when they are general rather than being too specific.

7. Weak attitudes predict behavior more successfully than strong ones.

8. When self-interest is involved, behavior cannot be predicted very well from attitudes.

9. A communicator will be better able to change peoples' attitudes if the audience thinks the message was deliberately meant to persuade them.

MATCHING ANSWERS:

1–C [135]; 2–E [136]; 3–H [136]; 4–B [141]; 5–A [129]; 6–D [140]; 7–F [122]; 8–G [146]

WHAT'S WRONG HERE? ANSWERS:

1. When subliminal photos caused negative affect, the strange was rated negatively; likewise, subliminal affect from positive photos also transferred to the stranger. [122]
2. Genetic factors seem to be more important in shaping gut-level attitude than cognitive ones. [124]
3. Attitudes based on direct experience generally affect behavior to a greater degree. [128]
4. They were seldom refused service, despite the fact most establishments said in writing that they would refuse service. [126-127]
5. The appropriate question is not whether attitudes predict behavior, but how and when they do so. [126]
6. Specific attitudes predict behavior more successfully if the behavior to be predicted is quite specific whereas general attitudes predict general behaviors. [130]
7. Strong attitudes are better at predicting behavior. [129]
8. When we have a vested interest, behavior is likely to follow from the attitude. [129]
9. When we are forewarned about a speaker's intention to persuade, we are less likely to be persuaded. [141]

TRUE–FALSE:

Indicate whether each of the following statements is true or false. If false, indicate why. Correct answers are found at the end of the exercise.

1. Research comparing the attitude similarity between identical–twin pairs and between nonidentical–twin pairs has supported the hypothesis that genetic factors play no role in shaping attitudes.

2. To say that an attitude is "heritable" means that it is usually formed through social learning.

3. The stronger an attitude is, the better it is able to predict behavior.

4. The "passive persuasion" researchers at Yale found that people who have expertise in matters related to their message are more persuasive than people who lack such expertise.

5. The Yale researchers found that it is always harder to persuade a person who is distracted from a message than someone paying full attention.

6. A speaker who is trying to persuade someone should present both sides of the issue if the target is already in agreement with the message.

7. The Yale researchers found that people who speak slowly are usually more persuasive than people who speak rapidly.

8. Fear-arousing messages generally have little persuasive impact.

9. Message recipients "on the peripheral route" are influenced more by heuristic cues than recipients on the central route.

10. When a message contains convincing arguments, subjects are just as likely to be influenced by these arguments on the peripheral route as on the central route.

11. When subjects perceive that influence attempts are unduly strong, feelings of reactance are often produced.

12. Negative attitude change seldom occurs under conditions that arouse reactance.

13. In the Festinger and Carlsmith (1959) experiment, the more money subjects were paid to tell another person how interesting a boring experiment was, the more the subjects believed what they had said.

14. When a person engages in attitude-discrepant behavior and has very good reasons for performing such actions, little dissonance is produced.

TRUE-FALSE ANSWERS:

1. False; because of the greater similarity in the attitudes of the identical-twin pairs, it has been concluded that genetics probably plays a role. [124]
2. False; a heritable attitude is one for which genetic factors are important. [124]
3. True. [129]
4. True. [135]
5. False; often the distracted person is easier to persuade. [135]
6. False; both sides should be presented if the audience is initially in disagreement. [135]
7. False; fast speakers were generally found to be more persuasive. [136]
8. False; fear is effective, especially if specific recommendations are provided. [136]
9. True. [137]
10. False; subjects on the central route are more persuaded by convincing messages. [137]
11. True. [140]
12. False; negative attitude change is often a result of reactance. [140]
13. False; the less subjects were paid, the more they believed what they had said. [148]
14. True. [147-148]

FILL IN THE BLANKS: A GUIDED REVIEW

Mentally fill in each of the blanks in the following section while covering the answers in the margin. Check each answer against the answer in the margin by uncovering as you go along.

1. If a child's mother displays negative emotion each time an attitude object is present, the child will probably learn to associate negative emotion with this object. The learning process involved here is _____.

   classical conditioning [121]

2. When children's attitudes are strengthened because parents reward them for expressing "correct" views, the learning process is _____.

   instrumental conditioning [122]

3. When children acquire attitudes merely by watching someone else's behavior, the learning process is _____.

   observational learning [122]

4. When we try to determine whether our view of social reality is correct by comparing what we believe with the beliefs of others, the process underlying our attitudes is _____.

   social comparison [123]

5. The person who uses mental shortcuts to determine his/her attitudes instead of engaging in careful thought about the issues involved is engaging in _____ processing.

   heuristic [136-137]

6. A persuader with strong arguments will be more effective if the target is motivated to think about the arguments fully. A highly motivated target is engaging in _____ processing.

   systematic [136]

7. The term that refers to uncomfortable feelings generated by inconsistency between attitudes or by inconsistencies between a person's actions and attitudes is _____.

   cognitive dissonance [144]

8. _____ theory predicts that the fewer reasons we have for engaging in counterattitudinal behavior, the more attitude change will follow this behavior.

   Cognitive dissonance [146-148]

9. The negative reaction that occurs when we think someone is trying to limit our personal freedom by forcing us to do what they want us to do is called _____.

   reactance [140]

10. Advance knowledge that one is to be the target of a persuasion attempt is called _____.

    forewarning [141]

11. When a person resists persuasion by directing her attention away from information that challenges her existing attitude, the person is showing _____.

    selective avoidance [141]

12. A person who actively seeks information that supports his attitudes while avoiding information that challenges his attitudes is engaged in _____.

    selective exposure [141]

13. Getting people to persuade others to engage in recommended actions while reminding them that they haven't always practiced what they're preaching causes feelings of _____.

    hypocrisy [149]

14. The three conditions necessary for the less-leads-to-more effect to occur are
    1) _____
    2) _____
    3) _____

1) freely choose to do attitude-discrepant act; 2) feel personal responsibility; 3) feel pay was deserved [148]

15. One reason we may engage in systematic processing of a persuasive message is because we want to hold correct views. In other words, we are motivated by _____.

accuracy [138]

16. A second reason we may engage in systematic processing is to hold views consistent with our own interests or our own self. In other words, our motivation is _____.

defensive [138]

17. A third reason we may engage in systematic processing is to hold attitudes that make us look good to others. In other words, we are motivated by _____.

impression formation [138]

18. When people evaluate information that disconfirms their existing views as less convincing and less reliable than information that confirms their existing views, they are engaging in _____.

biased assimilation [141-142]

19. When people evaluate mixed evidence in such a way that is actually strengthens their preexisting view, making it more extreme than before, they are showing _____.

attitude polarization [142]

MULTIPLE–CHOICE QUESTIONS: A PERSONAL QUIZ

After you have finished reading the chapter and done the other exercises in the STUDY GUIDE, take the quiz found below to test your knowledge. Indicate your answers by circling the letter of the chosen alternative. Check your answers against the answers provided at the end of the exercise.

1. When affect–inducing photographs were presented subliminally, just before pictures of a person, the effect on attitudes toward the person was
   a. to modify the affective component despite subjects' not realizing the presence of the photographs.
   b. to modify the affective component only among subjects aware of the contents of the photographs.
   c. no change in the affective component occurred.
   d. to make the person more identifiable, although attitudes remained unchanged.

2. Compared to attitudes acquired through indirect experience, attitudes acquired through direct experience
   a. are the basis for slower, more deliberate responses.
   b. exert stronger effects on behavior.
   c. are held with less confidence.
   d. are weaker.

3. Studies of similarity in attitudes among twin pairs has found that
   a. identical twins hold attitudes no more similar to one another than fraternal twins.
   b. identical twins hold attitudes that are more similar to one another than fraternal twins; this finding supports the genetic view of attitudes.
   c. identical twins hold attitudes that are more similar to one another than fraternal twins; this finding supports the environmental view of attitudes.
   d. fraternal twins hold attitudes that are more similar to one another than identical twins; this finding supports the genetic view of attitudes.

4. When LaPiere examined questionnaire responses and behavioral responses of restaurants to a touring Chinese couple in the 1930s, he found that most restaurants
   a. indicated in writing they'd serve a Chinese couple and actually served them.
   b. indicated in writing they wouldn't serve a Chinese couple, and they didn't.
   c. indicated in writing they'd serve a Chinese couple but refused service.
   d. indicated in writing they wouldn't serve a Chinese couple but actually served them

5. Which of the following is true?
   a. Accurate predictions of overt behavior can often be derived from people's specific attitudes.
   b. Attitudes formed as a result of direct experience with the attitude object are poor predictors of behavior.
   c. The more general the attitudes involved, the greater the accuracy in predicting particular behaviors.
   d. The best conclusion is that attitudes do not predict behavior.

6. Whether a student will actually undergo body piercing to wear a nose ornament is best predicted by the _____; how someone reacts to a panhandler who approaches them on the street is best predicted by the _____.
   a. theory of planned behavior; attitude-to-behavior process model
   b. attitude-to-behavior process model; theory of planned behavior
   c. theory of planned behavior; theory of planned behavior also
   d. attitude-to-behavior process model; attitude-to-behavior process model also

7. A person who is trying to persuade us will be better able to produce attitude change if he
   a. speaks rapidly and doesn't deliberately set out to persuade us.
   b. speaks slowly and doesn't deliberately set out to persuade us.
   c. speaks rapidly and deliberately sets out to persuade us.
   d. speaks slowly and deliberately sets out to persuade us.

8. Which of the following is *not* a finding reported by the researchers who studied persuasion using the Yale approach?
   a. Experts are more persuasive than nonexperts.
   b. People who speak slowly are more persuasive than people who speak rapidly.
   c. Persuasion can be enhanced by fear-arousing messages.
   d. It is sometimes easier to persuade a person who is distracted from a message than one paying full attention.

9. When attitudes are changed without careful thought about the issue or the arguments being used, the persuasion route being used is the _____ route.
   a. peripheral
   b. central
   c. elaborative
   d. heuristic

10. According to the elaboration likelihood model, a persuader with strong, convincing arguments should use the _____ route.
    a. peripheral
    b. central
    c. elaborative
    d. heuristic

11. Which is true regarding persuasion on the peripheral route?
    a. produces long-lasting, permanent attitude change
    b. attitude change results from careful processing of information in the message
    c. attitude change depends on presence of persuasion cues
    d. is especially likely when message is relevant to receiver

12. If an attitude helps a person to organize and interpret diverse information, the attitude is serving a _____ function.
    a. self-identity
    b. self-esteem
    c. knowledge
    d. self-expression

13. When people resist attempts to persuade them by directing their attention away from information that challenges their existing attitudes, their resistance to persuasion is based on
    a. reactance.
    b. forewarning.
    c. biased assimilation.
    d. selective avoidance.

14. Which of the following is an example of biased assimilation found in the Munro and Ditto (1997) study?
    a. High-prejudice persons were more convinced by information about homosexuals presented in the study.
    b. Low-prejudice persons were more convinced by information about homosexuals presented in the study.
    c. Low-prejudice persons found stereotyped information about homosexuals to be more convincing.
    d. Low-prejudice persons found nonsterotyped information about homosexuals to be more convincing.

15. Which of the following conclusions is true?
    a. There is evidence that dissonance is both arousing and unpleasant.
    b. While dissonance is arousing, it is not unpleasant.
    c. While dissonance is unpleasant, it is not arousing.
    d. Dissonance is neither unpleasant nor arousing.

16. The negative reaction which occurs when we perceive that someone is trying to limit our personal freedom is called
    a. dissonance.
    b. reactance.
    c. discrepancy.
    d. fogging.

17. Which of the following is a way to reduce dissonance following induced compliance?
    a. Increase the perceived importance of the inconsistency.
    b. Change attitudes to make them inconsistent with the behavior.
    c. Change cognitions to make them inconsistent with the behavior.
    d. Conclude that the attitudes or behaviors in question don't really matter.

18. Which of the following is an example of the use of hypocrisy as a way to modify attitudes?
    a. Get people to say something they don't believe.
    b. Get people to encourage others to do some beneficial action, then remind them that they don't always do it themselves.
    c. Simply get people to encourage others to do some beneficial action.
    d. Simply remind people that they don't always perform beneficial actions.

MULTIPLE–CHOICE ANSWERS

1. a [122]	6. a [131-132]	11. c [136-139]	16. b [140]
2. b [128]	7. a [135-136]	12. c [138]	17. d [144]
3. b [124]	8. b [135-136]	13. d [141]	18. b [149-150]
4. d [126-127]	9. a [136]	14. d [141-143]	
5. a [130]	10. b [137-139]	15. a [145-146]	

IF YOU'D LIKE TO KNOW MORE: FURTHER SOURCES OF INFORMATION

Poindexter, J. (1983, August). Voices of Authority. PSYCHOLOGY TODAY, 53-61. Lee Iacocca, and other chief executives of U.S. corporations, seem to be succeeding as communicators in advertising. This article examines why.

Benson, P. L. (1981, December). Religion on Capitol Hill: How Beliefs Affect Voting Behavior in the U.S. Congress. PSYCHOLOGY TODAY, 47-57. An interesting examination of the attitude/behavior relationship.

MacLachlan, J. (1979, November). What People Really Think of Fast Talkers. PSYCHOLOGY TODAY, 112-117. Fast-talking salesmen seem slippery and shallow, right? Wrong! Studies conclude that faster is often regarded as more intelligent and convincing.

Moine, D. J. (1983, August). To Trust, Perchance to Buy. PSYCHOLOGY TODAY, 51. Suggests that the best persuaders mirror customer's thoughts, tone of voice, speech tempo, and mood.

Keating, John P. (1971, April). A Politician's Guide to Success on the Stump: Hire a Heckler. PSYCHOLOGY TODAY, 70. Does a speaker have a better chance of getting his message through to his audience when the audience is distracted? Several theories say "yes."

Go to http://depts.washington.edu/iat/ Do people speak their minds? Do people know their minds? This web site presents a new method called the Implicit Association Test (IAT for short) that is supposed to help us answer these questions.

Go to http://www.lafayette.edu/mcglonem/prop.html   This site examines the use of propaganda to wage psychological warfare. Links are provided to contemporary Fascist propaganda, holocaust revisionist propaganda, U.S. political propaganda, and religious propaganda.

Go to http://www.pg.dk/pg/advertising/index.html   This site shares knowledge about advertising on the Web. The Internet and the Web are communication media which are growing dramatically and thus need to be taken seriously.

THINKING CRITICALLY ABOUT ATTITUDES

1. Think of some topic or issue that is important to you. Perhaps it's a social issue like gun control, health care for the elderly, abortion, or welfare spending. Or perhaps it's a more personal issue, such as your attitude toward your high school or your attitude toward one of your relatives. Whatever issue you settle on, think about the people and the experiences you've had that have contributed to your attitude. Can you think of people who've been especially influential in shaping attitudes? Can you think of experiences where you've been classically conditioned? Can you think of other instances that relate to the coverage of attitudes in chapter four?

2. Attempt to analyze the persuasion techniques used in newspapers and magazines. Can you find advertisements that seem to be based on the traditional approach to persuasion presented on pages 135-136 of your textbook? Can you find, for example, an ad that uses an expert communicator? Can you find one that uses communicator attractiveness as the basis of the appeal? Or, can you find an ad that seems to have hidden its intent to persuade us, as might be suggested by point 2 on page 135. Still another possibility is to find emotional appeals, such as the fear-inducing appeals discussed on page 136 of the text. Perhaps your instructor would encourage class members to share interesting examples with the class.

3. Another topic you can understand better by finding examples from your everyday experience is the elaboration likelihood model. The chapter gives you a detailed description of the differences between the central and peripheral routes to persuasion on pages 136-137. Can you think of television ads that use the two routes? The ads using the central route are presented directly to the viewer, whereas ads using the peripheral route are often embedded in distraction. Are the ads using the central route based on better-quality arguments than those using the peripheral route? Can you identify any persuasion cues in ads where the peripheral route is being used? A way to share interesting examples might be for you to record them with a VCR and ask your instructor if he/she would allow you to share them with the class.

4. To what degree do you trust a used car salesman? To what degree do you trust a physician or a dentist? To what degree do you trust a college professor or a politician? Now that you've briefly considered the trustworthiness of these occupations, try to explain the basis for your opinion. What characteristics do you associate with trustworthiness? Why are some occupations considered to be low in trustworthiness? Do you think credibility depends on a communicator's occupational category?

ASPECTS OF SOCIAL IDENTITY:
SELF AND GENDER

CHAPTER OUTLINE: GETTING THE OVERALL PICTURE:

Before reading the chapter, it may be helpful to examine the chapter outline. This will give you an idea of what is covered in the chapter and should help you organize your learning and review the material. You can also record notes on text sections under the outline headings for those sections.

I. The Self: Components of One's Identity

    A. Self-Concept: The All-Important Schema

        1. The Content of a Person's Self Concept

        2. The Cognitive Effects of a Person's Self-Schema

        3. How Is the Self-Concept Structured?

        4. One Self-Concept or Many?

        5. Changing the Self-Concept

    B. Social Diversity: A Critical Analysis—Cultural Influences on the Self: The Effects of Individualism versus Collectivism

    C. Self-Esteem: Attitudes about Oneself

        1. Self-Evaluations

        2. Self-Esteem and Social Comparison

        3. The Effects of Having High versus Low Self-Esteem

        4. Variable Self-Esteem

    D. Cornerstones of Social Psychology: Rogers, Self-Theory, Self-Ideal Discrepancy, and Personality Change

II. Other Aspects of Self-Functioning: Focusing, Monitoring, and Efficacy

    A. Focusing on Oneself versus Focusing on the External World

        1. Cognitive and Affective Aspects of Focusing on Self

        2. Storing Positive and Negative Information about Self in Memory

    B. Monitoring One's Behavior on the Basis of Internal Versus External Factors

        1. Monitoring as a Dispositional Factor

        2. Other Behaviors Associated with Differences in Self-Monitoring

    C. Self-Efficacy: Having Confidence in Oneself

        1. Performance as a Function of Self-Efficacy

        2. The Effect of Self-Efficacy on Interpersonal Behavior

        3. Increases in Feelings of Efficacy

III. Gender: Maleness or Femaleness As a Crucial Aspect of Identity

    A. Gender Identity and Gender Stereotypes

        1. The Development of One's Gender Identity

        2. What Is the Basis of Gender Identity?

        3. Psychological Androgyny As an Alternative to Masculinity and Femininity

    B. Gender-Role Behavior and Reactions to Gender-Role Behavior

        1. Androgynous versus Gender-Typed Behavior

        2. Effects of Gender Roles on Behavior

        3. Why Are Traditional Gender Roles Still Powerful?

        4. Encouraging Signs of Progress in Moving beyond Gender Stereotypes

    C. Beyond the Headlines: As Social Psychologists See It—Does Gender Discrimination Still Occur in the Workplace?

    D. When Men and Women Differ: Biology, Gender Roles, or Both?

1. Differences in the Interpersonal Behavior of Males and Females

2. Differences in the Self-Perceptions of Males and Females

LEARNING OBJECTIVES: WHAT YOU SHOULD LEARN

As you are reading the chapter, these objectives provide page-by-page questions for you to answer. Answering the objectives should assure that you understand the essential material in the chapter.

1. Examine evidence that our self-concept is determined by genetics as well as by social context, and examine the types of self-awareness found in animals and humans. [159-160]

2. What is meant by the statement that each person possesses a unique self-concept with specific content, but that the overall structure of the self-concept is the same across individuals? [160]

3. Describe the self-reference effect, and understand how recall of self-relevant information is facilitated by elaborative processing and by categorical processing. [161-163]

4. Examine the structure of the self-concept, including central vs. peripheral self-conceptions, self-concept clarity, sexual self-schema, and the social self-concept. [153-165]

5. Describe cultural influences on the self-concept, by comparing collectivistic cultures with individualistic cultures. [165-166]

6. Compare the concepts of present self, future self, and possible selves, and summarize advantages of being able to envision many possible selves. [167-168]

7. Examine how life events influence our self-concept, including the reciprocal process between roommates and the idea that we hold role-specific self-concepts. [168-169]

8. Define the concept of self-esteem, and understand the three possible motives for self-evaluation. [169-170]

9. How do the following aspects of self-evaluations affect us? a) cultural differences; b) having negative self-esteem; c) whether negative self-evaluations are specific or global; and d) having a discrepancy between self and ideal self. [170-171]

10. Describe circumstances in which social comparisons lead to increases in self-esteem, and also circumstances in which social comparisons lead to decreases in self-esteem. [171-173]

11. Examine consequences of having high vs. low self-esteem, and also the consequences of having variable self-esteem. [173; 175]

12. Understand Rogers' view of maladaptive self-perceptions, and describe how and why his therapy deals with self-ideal discrepancy. [174-175]

13. Describe circumstances that increase self-focusing and effects created when we become self-focused. [176-177]

14. Compare effects created by compartmentalized versus evaluatively integrated self-organization. [177-179]

15. Describe high and low self-monitors and indicate the various ways in which the behavior of high and low self-monitors is different. [179-181]

16. Define self-efficacy, and note how it is related to physical performance, academic performance, job performance among physicians, interpersonal behavior, and coping with phobias. [182-185]

17. Thing about the origins of gender differences, and describe stages children go through in the process of developing gender identity. [185-187]

18. Discuss the implications of sex typing and describe ways in which infants and children develop gender-appropriate behavior. [187-189]

19. Describe the Bem Sex Role Inventory and the assumptions underlying it, and indicate characteristics of persons who are masculine, feminine, androgynous, and undifferentiated. [188-190]

20. Summarize advantages that accrue to individuals who are androgynous, and describe problems often associated with strong adherence to traditional sex roles. [191-192]

21. Compare gender role behaviors of men and women within the home and in the workplace, and examine how gender affects expectancies regarding performance and success. [192-193]

22. Examine gender discrimination in the U. S. State Department, and also understand gender differences in academia, in communication styles, in hiring practices, and in pay for male-dominated vs. female-dominated professions. [193-195]

23. Give examples where cultural support is provided for traditional gender roles in religious writings, children's stories, movies, and television, as well as examples demonstrating movement away from traditional gender roles. [195-198]

24. Describe the role of testosterone in producing dominating and controlling behavior, and examine the role of learning in producing differences between women and men. [199-200]

25. Describe the differences between women and men in the degree to which their self-perceptions are based on appearance. [200-202]

26. Compare Causasian women's concern about weight with the concern expressed by Asian and Black women. [202]

There's More Than First Meets Your Eyes: Understanding Figures in Your Text

Turn to the following figure in your text and follow the discussion about how the figure can increase you understanding of research and theory.

1. Figure 5.8 (page 175) summarizes one of the central assumptions underlying Carl Rogers' theory of personality. Rogers assumes that a psychologically healthy person views his actual self to be close to what he would ideally like to be. Since the goal of therapy is to create a more psychologically healthy client, the goal can also be seen as reducing the difference (the "discrepancy") between the actual self and the ideal self. Those clients who "improve" show an ideal self that is closer to the actual self than before they entered therapy. Control subjects who are not in therapy continue to show the discrepancy between the ideal self and the actual self.

KEY TERMS: CONCEPTS YOU NEED TO UNDERSTAND

Write out the meaning of the following terms in your own words. Cover the right-hand portion of the exercise until you have finished, then check on the accuracy of your answers by comparing them with the definitions provided.

1.	self-concept	our organized collection of beliefs about ourselves including meaningful past experiences, knowledge of what we are like now, and expectancies about future changes [160-161]
2.	self-esteem	the evaluation an individual makes of himself, varying from good, capable, and worthy (positive self-esteem) to useless, inept, and unworthy (negative self-esteem) [169]
3.	self-focusing	the act of directing attention inward to one's self [176]
4.	self-monitoring	the degree to which individuals regulate their behavior on the basis of external situations (high self-monitors) or on the basis of internal factors such as their own beliefs, attitudes, and interests (low self-monitors) [179]
5.	self-efficacy	a person's perception of his or her ability or competency to deal with a given task or to reach a goal [182]
6.	gender identity	the "maleness," or "femaleness" that a person associates with himself or herself; most commonly, people identify themselves with characteristics associated with their biological sex [186]
7.	androgyny	term for those whose self-descriptions include elements consistent with both traditional masculine and traditional feminine gender roles [188-189]
8.	traditional gender roles	expectations that accrue to people based on whether they are male or female [195]

MATCHING:

Match each concept on the left of the next page with an identifying phrase, word or sentence on the right side of the page. The answers may be found immediately after this section.

A.	concerned about appearance	__	1.	organized collection of beliefs
B.	self-reference effect	__	2.	open to change
C.	self-schema	__	3.	pushes me to seek accurate self-knowledge
D.	BSRI	__	4.	exaggerated expression of the traditional male role
E.	working self-concept	__	5.	especially likely among women
F.	self-assessment motive	__	6.	causes me to easily recall information related to myself
G.	hypermasculinity	__	7.	pushes me to seek favorable self-knowledge
H.	self-enhancement motive	__	8.	measures whether person is sex typed

MATCHING ANSWERS:

1–C [160]; 2–E [167]; 3–F [170]; 4–G [192]; 5–A [200-202]; 6–B [162]; 7–H [170]; 8–D [190]

WHAT'S WRONG HERE?

For each statement below indicate what is needs to be changed in order to make the statement correct. You will find the answers at the end of the exercise, along with pages in the text where you can find more information.

1. Rentsch and Heffner (1994) concluded that each person possesses a unique self-concept, with the categories used to describe themselves being different for each individual as well as the specific content mentioned within categories.

2. The text concludes that the self–reference effect is caused exclusively by the fact that self–related words are processed more elaborately than words unrelated to the self.

3. Cross-cultural research concludes that there is no difference between Americans and Japanese in the degree to which they show self-enhancement and self-criticism.

4. Teaching Mexican-American children in grades 3-5 to have an expanded view of the future possibilities in their lives had no effect on their understanding of the relevance of school to their future success.

5. McNulty and Swann (1994) suggested that by the time college students enter into an interpersonal relationship with a new roommate, their self-concept is so well established that it is virtually impossible for the roommate to affect it.

6. Women asked to describe themselves in different roles displayed role-specific self-concepts with no consistency within the individual as she moved from role to role.

7. When given an opportunity to gain knowledge about ourselves, we often seek self-assessment and self-enhancement, but self-verification is seldom seen.

8. Research has supported the idea that it is better in the long run for a person to have unrealistically positive self-esteem than to make accurate self-evaluations.

9. A person who regulates his behavior on the basis of internal factors such as beliefs, attitudes, and values would score high in self-monitoring.

10. Feelings of self–efficacy readily generalize from one situation to another.

11. People low in self–efficacy perform tasks just as well as people high in self–efficacy.

12. The text considers sex and gender to be the same concept.

13. The BSRI assumes that people have either masculine or feminine characteristics, but it is considered impossible to have both.

WHAT'S WRONG HERE? ANSWERS:

1. While the specific content mentioned within categories is unique, Rentsch and Heffner determined that there are eight basic categories people use. [160-161]
2. The text presents evidence that both elaborative and categorical processing are involved. [162-163]
3. Americans more often show self-enhancement, while Japanese more often show self-criticism. [165-166]
4. In fact, these children were improved in their understanding of what it means to be a good student and saw connections with future job opportunities. [168]
5. The authors suggest the feedback we get from others alters how we conceptualize the self. [160]
6. There is change in self concept as women change from one role to the next, but there is also evidence for consistency across roles. [169]
7. All three motives are active, even including the tendency to self-verify negative information about oneself. [170]
8. While unrealistically positive self-esteem can have temporary benefits, accurate self-evaluation is better in the long run. [173]
9. This describes a person who is a low self-monitor. [179]
10. Self-efficacy is quite situation–specific. [182]
11. People high in self–efficacy perform better in a wide range of tasks. [182]

12. Sex refers to whether one is a male or a female; gender refers to the degree to which one is masculine or feminine. [185]

13. A common theme in research is that androgyny is preferred over both traditional masculinity and traditional femininity. [189-191]

TRUE–FALSE:

Indicate whether each of the following statements is true or false. If false, indicate why. Correct answers are found at the end of the exercise.

1. An athlete who identifies strongly and exclusively with the role of athlete is more emotionally upset by an athletic injury than an athlete with a variety of possible future selves.

2. When we compare ourselves to someone we don't know very well who is worse off than ourselves, it raises our self-esteem.

3. Rogers found that persons who have a large self-ideal discrepancy generally have high self-esteem.

4. According to Butler, Hokanson, and Flynn (1994), variable self-esteem is a better indicator that someone will become depressed than low self-esteem.

5. High self–monitors vary their behavior depending on the specific situation or audience, whereas low self–monitors behave more consistently with less regard for the situation.

6. The fact that identical twins answer some questions related to self-monitoring more similarly than fraternal twins has been interpreted as evidence that self-monitoring is partly based on genetic factors.

7. High self–monitors tend to select a companion on the basis of how well the person performs, while low self–monitors tend to select the companion on the basis of how much they like the person.

8. People with high social self–efficacy who receive negative feedback after a social exchange conclude that it's their fault.

9. Whether people were frightened by a tarantula spider in the Riskind and Maddux (1993) study depended solely on whether the spider was moving toward or moving away from them.

10. Hypermasculinity is considered to be the ideal gender-role identification for a male.

11. Men and women who are found to be "androgynous" on the BSRI do not divide up the work around the house along traditional gender lines.

12. Men and women show an equivalent level of concern over what the salary is for a particular job.

TRUE–FALSE ANSWERS:

1. True. [167]
2. True. [172]
3. False; a large self-ideal discrepancy is associated with low self-esteem. [174]
4. True. [175]
5. True. [179]
6. True. [181]
7. True. [180]
8. False; those with high self–efficacy attribute the feedback to something about the situation. [182-183]
9. False; the only people frightened by the tarantula were those with low self-efficacy who saw it approaching them. [184-185]
10. False; researchers consider hypermasculinity to be an undesirable gender type. [192]
11. False; even androgynous men and women follow the culturally prescribed gender roles. [192]
12. False; men show a greater concern with salary, whereas women express concern about whether the job would be personally satisfying. [193]

FILL IN THE BLANKS: A GUIDED REVIEW

Mentally fill in each of the blanks in the following section while covering the answers in the margin. Check each answer against the answer in the margin by uncovering as you go along.

1.	The tendency for information related to the self to be more readily processed and remembered than other information is known as the _____ effect.	self-reference [161]
2.	When we remember words because we have spent considerable time thinking about them, which thereby connects these words to existing information in memory, we have processed the words via _____ processing.	elaborative [162]
3.	When we remember words because we have organized them by placing them in categories already present in our memories, we have processed the words using _____ processing.	categorical [163]
4.	Since the self-concept I currently have is open to change in response to new experiences and new information, it is best to think of my current self-concept as a _____.	working self-concept [167]
5.	Passionate-romantic, open-direct, and embarrassed-conservative are the three major components of our _____.	sexual self-schema [163]
6.	Mental representations of what we might become as we change in the future are referred to as _____.	possible selves [167]
7.	Self evaluations, ranging from positive to negative, make up the attitudinal dimension known as _____.	self-esteem [169]

8. A woman who conceptualizes herself differently depending on whether she's thinking of herself as mother, wife, or worker is demonstrating _____.

role-specific self-concepts [169-170]

9. Social comparison with someone who is worse off than you are is referred to as _____.

downward comparison [172]

10. The difference between a person's self-concept and the person's conception of an ideal self is known as _____.

self-ideal discrepancy [172]

11. Carl Rogers' therapy technique in which the therapist is interested, accepting, and non-judgmental in order to create an atmosphere where the client can explore his actual feelings is _____.

client-centered therapy [174]

12. Persons who tailor their behavior to specific situations and audiences are _____ self-monitors; persons who behave in the same way, regardless or the situation are _____ self-monitors.

high; low [179-180]

13. The therapy technique in which participants are gradually taught over a series of trials to relax in the presence of snake cues and thereby develop a sense of self-efficacy is _____.

desensitization [184]

14. When a person reacts to a feared object with the perception he has the ability to prevent himself from being harmed, he is reacting with feelings of _____.

self-efficacy [182-184]

15. The term that refers to the biologically-based differences between males and females that develop on the basis of genes present at conception is _____; the term _____ refers to the personality characteristics, actions, expectancies, and other attributes that are typical of women or men in a particular society.

sex; gender [185]

16. Between the ages of four and seven, children acquire the principles of _____, which means that they realize that gender is a basic attribute of a person that remains constant over time.

gender consistency [186]

17. A person responding to Bem's Sex Role Inventory who scores high on both masculinity and femininity is said to be _____.

androgynous [189]

18. A person responding to Bem's Sex Role Inventory who scores low on both masculinity and femininity is said to be _____ with respect to gender roles.

undifferentiated [190]

19. An extreme gender-role identification with an exaggerated version of the traditional female role is called _____.

hyperfemininity [192]

20. The hormone, found in higher levels in males than in females, that has been linked to the tendency to dominate and to control is _____.

testosterone [199]

21. The female "sex hormone," secreted by the ovaries is _____.

estrogen [199]

MULTIPLE-CHOICE QUESTIONS: A PERSONAL QUIZ

After you have finished reading the chapter and done the other exercises in the STUDY GUIDE, take the quiz found below to test your knowledge. Indicate your answers by circling the letter of the chosen alternative. Check your answers against the answers provided at the end of the exercise.

1. When information is relevant to the self
   a. we are likely to engage in elaborative processing.
   b. we are likely to engage in categorical processing.
   c. the information is difficult to enter into memory.
   d. both a and b.

2. The fact that information about the self is more readily processed and remembered than other information is called the
   a. self-efficacy effect.
   b. self-focusing effect.
   c. self-monitoring effect.
   d. self-reference effect.

3. Persons most vulnerable to feedback indicating they lack necessary skills to enter their chosen profession are those who have
   a. a complex view of their possible selves.
   b. a limited number of possible future selves.
   c. possible selves that are unrealistically grounded.
   d. cultural taboos about thinking too much about the future.

4. Researchers working with young Mexican American students tried to improve school performance and career orientation by
   a. getting them to focus on a more narrow view of themselves.
   b. helping them develop greater pride in their Hispanic heritage.
   c. getting them to consider multiple future careers and showing them that school is relevant to careers.
   d. developing a strong social identity in place of their individual identities.

5. Which is true regarding role-specific self-concepts and general self-concepts?
   a. Role-specific self-concepts change from role to role, but the general self-concept is more consistent.
   b. The general self-concept changes from moment to moment, but the role-specific self-concept is fixed.
   c. Neither self-concept is very consistent.
   d. Both self-concepts change from moment to moment.

6. "Self-evaluations made along a positive-negative dimension." This refers to
   a. self-esteem.
   b. self-concept.
   c. self-schema.
   d. self-monitoring.

7. A downward comparison with someone who is very close to oneself
   a. raises self-esteem.
   b. does not influence self-esteem.
   c. produces a contrast effect.
   d. has a negative effect on self-esteem.

8. A person who is very competent but has unrealistically negative self-esteem is referred to by the term
   a. evaluatively-integrated self-organization.
   b. compartmentalized self-organization.
   c. variable self-esteem.
   d. paradoxical self-esteem.

9. Which clients have the smallest self-ideal discrepancy?
   a. Troubled clients who have not undergone therapy.
   b. Initially troubled clients who have undergone 6-12 months of client-centered therapy.
   c. Initially troubled clients who show definite improvement during 6-12 months of client-centered therapy.
   d. None of the above; self-ideal discrepancy is not related to therapy.

10. Which of the following persons is most likely to become depressed?
    a. an individual with low self-esteem.
    b. an individual with variable self-esteem.
    c. an individual with high self-esteem.
    d. None of the above; depression and self-esteem are not related.

11. Compared with low self-monitors, high self-monitors have been shown to
    a. vary less in their behavior from situation to situation.
    b. rate advertised products more positively after seeing a quality-based ad.
    c. select a companion based on how much they like the other person.
    d. speak more often in the third person.

12. Compared to persons low in self-efficacy, persons high in self-efficacy have been shown to
    a. be less successful as professors in completing research projects.
    b. have less endurance in exercise involving physical endurance.
    c. fall short of their own expectancies regarding performance.
    d. be more efficient and more effective physicians.

13. After receiving negative feedback regarding their performance in a social situation, persons with low social self–efficacy interpret the performance in terms of
    a. something about the situation.
    b. their deficient social skills.
    c. their lack of self–efficacy.
    d. a and b are equally likely.

14. Riskind and Maddux (1993) found that fear of a tarantula spider was triggered when the spider
    a. moved closer to a person with low self-efficacy.
    b. moved closer to a person with high self-efficacy.
    c. moved away from a person with low self-efficacy.
    d. both a and b

15. Which of the following is true?
    a. Children become aware of their own sex or gender at the same time they acquire principles of gender consistency.
    b. Children acquire principles of gender consistency before they become aware of their own sex or gender.
    c. Children become aware of their own sex or gender before they acquire principles of gender consistency.
    d. There is no consistent relationship between becoming aware of one's sex and acquiring principles of gender consistency.

16. Which of the following persons is (are) androgynous?
    a. a person who scores high on both the masculine and feminine scales of the BSRI
    b. a person who scores low on both the masculine and feminine scales of the BSRI
    c. a male who scores high on the feminine scale but low on the masculine scale of the BSRI
    d. both a and b

17. Which of these involves extreme gender-role identification with the female role?
    a. the traditional female role
    b. androgyny
    c. hyperfeminity
    d. subjective self-awareness

18. High levels of testosterone are associated with
    a. a submissive style of behavior in groups.
    b. high verbal skills.
    c. low sociability.
    d. dominance behaviors.

19. When an overweight woman is evaluated negatively in the workplace,
    a. she rejects the evaluation as showing unfair bias by the evaluator.
    b. she is as likely as an overweight male to internalize the evaluation.
    c. she is less likely than an overweight male to internalize the evaluation.
    d. she feels that the negative evaluation is justified.

20. Who is most likely to judge themselves as being overweight and to evaluate their bodies negatively?
    a. Asian women
    b. African-American women
    c. Caucasian women
    d. None of the above; women of all groups show the same level of concern over weight.

MULTIPLE–CHOICE ANSWERS

1. d [162-163]	6. a [169]	11. d [180]	16. a [189-190]
2. d [161]	7. d [172]	12. d [182-183]	17. c [192]
3. b [167]	8. d [173]	13. b [182-183]	18. d [199]
4. c [168]	9. c [174-175]	14. a [184-185]	19. a [201]
5. a [169]	10. b [175]	15. c [186]	20. c [202]

IF YOU'D LIKE TO KNOW MORE: FURTHER SOURCES OF INFORMATION

Roberts, M. (1988, February). School Yard Menace. PSYCHOLOGY TODAY, 52–56. Is bullying a personality trait? Or does the school yard bring out meanness in some children? Bullies are usually boys and usually come from families that neglect, reject, abuse children, or create an environment of violence.

Trotter, R. J. (1987, February). Stop Blaming Yourself. PSYCHOLOGY TODAY, 31–39. The title says it all. People whose explanatory style reflects learned helplessness blame themselves and suffer the health consequences.

Horn, J. (1986, March). Measuring a Man by the Company He Keeps. PSYCHOLOGY TODAY, 12. Mark Snyder, Ellen Berscheid and Peter Glick asked high and low self–monitors what kind of information they wanted about potential dates. The lows went for personality information and the highs for physical attractiveness profiles.

The Modern Prince. (1983). PSYCHOLOGY TODAY, a special section beginning in 1983. Niccolo Machiavelli was an Italian statesman who believed in manipulating other people (there is even a psychological scale named after him). One would well be wary of such a personality. You can learn all about Machiavellian types, and have a few laughs while you're at it, by following The Modern Prince.

Bower, B. (1985, August 31). Childhood Origins of Type A Behavior. SCIENCE NEWS, 133. Type A behaviors begins early. Children with the A pattern show more physical symptoms associated with stress and more sleep disturbances.

Salvatore, D. (1983, April). Young Feminists Speaking for Themselves. MS. 43. With the changes in society, the personalities of individual women are becoming more complex and more unique. On the cutting edge of that change are the young feminists. It would be a good idea for young men to read this article....and young women too.

Go to http://metalab.unc.edu/cheryb/women/wresources.html   This site, called Women's Resources on the Internet, provides links to a variety of information by and about women.

Go to http://web.indstate.edu.spsmm/   This is the home page for the Society for the Psychology Study of Men and Masculinity. The purpose of the society is "to promote the critical study of how gender shapes and constricts men's lives and to enhance men's capacity to experience their full human potential."

Go to http://www.wfu.edu/~leary/self/self.htm   This is the home page for a scholarly association called the International Society for Self and Identity.

Go to http://www.selfgrowth.com/   This page provides links to "self improvement." The primary focus of the page is to provide people with motivational and inspirational quotes that will bring them happiness and peace of mind.

THINKING CRITICALLY ABOUT SOCIAL IDENTITY

1. Personality theorists and social psychologists often disagree on the relative importance of personality traits versus situations as the determinants of behavior. Personality theorists examine the effect of individual differences on behavior, emphasizing ways in which different people behave differently from one another. Social psychologists, on the other hand, examine ways in which particular situations cause most people to behave the same. Consider, for example, the characteristic of shyness. Is shyness a personality trait, with some people being very shy and others less shy? Or is shyness a common response to certain situations, with most people becoming shy if the situation is "right"? Perhaps the choice you make indicates whether you're a social psychologist or a personality psychologist.

2. The previous critical thinking topic oversimplifies the personality versus situation issue. The best conclusion is undoubtedly that both personality and the situation are important. Chapter 5 implicitly makes this assumption. Several aspects of the self are discussed, first as trait features and then as situationally-determined features. Self-esteem, self-efficacy, and self-focusing are all discussed in this way. Later, in chapter 7, your text considers affiliation in both ways as well, discussing need for affiliation as a disposition and then discussing it as a response to "external events."

3. Does positive self-esteem involve overestimating positive aspects of yourself? People who claim unrealistically positive aspects of themselves generally score higher on self-esteem scales. Likewise, those who admit to negative aspects of themselves will score lower. The question to ponder is the degree to which positive self-esteem is based on a realistic view of oneself and the degree to which it is based on unrealistic positive views.

4. Do you want to do a simple demonstration of the self-reference effect? All you need to do is prepare a list of trait words and then present them to several of your friends, with two different instructions. One group should read the traits, indicating with a yes or no response whether each trait describes them. The other group should read the traits, indicating with a yes or no response

whether each trait word contains the letter "e". After your friends go through the entire list of traits, give them a surprise recall test to see how many of the trait words they can recall. Participants who relate the words to themselves should process the words more deeply than participants who simply respond to a physical feature of the words, and therefore these participants should recall more of the words. A list of thirteen words to use in doing the exercise is as follows: aggressive, intelligent, friendly, superstitious, quiet, sentimental, bold, athletic, persistent, trusting, sensitive, energetic, shy.

5. How does "what happens to you" influence your view of yourself? Suppose your apartment is broken into and ransacked. Suppose that you get soaking wet in a thunderstorm on your way to class. Suppose your boyfriend or girlfriend breaks off a long-term relationship. To what degree would these kinds of things happening to you influence your self-esteem? Likewise, imagine you just obtained the dream job you've been planning for. Or suppose that you learn that you've won a large sum of money in the lottery. Would these kinds of events influence your self-esteem?

6

PREJUDICE AND DISCRIMINATION: UNDERSTANDING THEIR NATURE AND COUNTERING THEIR EFFECTS

CHAPTER OUTLINE: GETTING THE OVERALL PICTURE

Before reading the chapter, it may be helpful to examine the chapter outline. This will give you an idea of what is covered in the chapter and should help you organize your learning and review the material. You can also record notes on text sections under the outline headings for those sections.

I. Prejudice and Discrimination: Their Nature and Effects

   A. Prejudice: Choosing Whom To Hate

   B. Discrimination: Prejudice in Action

      1. The New Racism: Subtle, but Just As Deadly

      2. Tokenism: Small Benefits, High Costs

      3. Reverse Discrimination: Giving with One Hand, Taking with the Other

II. The Origins of Prejudice: Contrasting Perspectives

   A. Direct Intergroup Conflict: Competition As a Source of Prejudice

   B. Cornerstones of Social Psychology—The Economics of Racial Violence: Do "Bad Times" Fan the Flames of Prejudice?

   C. Early Experience: The Role of Social Learning

   D. Social Categorization: The Us-versus-Them Effect and the "Ultimate" Attribution Error

   E. Social Diversity : A Critical Analysis: Perceived Similarity to Out-groups: Russians' reactions to Ukrainians, Moldavians, and Georgians

   F. Cognitive Sources of Prejudice: The Role of Stereotypes

      1. Stereotypes: What They Are And How They Operate

      2. Stereotypes and Prejudice

G. Other Cognitive Mechanisms in Prejudice: Illusory Correlations and Outgroup Homogeneity

    1. Ingroup Differentiation, Outgroup Homogeneity: "They're All the Same"—Or Are They?

III. Why Prejudice is Not Inevitable: Techniques for Countering its Effects

A. Breaking The Cycle of Prejudice: On Learning *Not* To Hate

B. Direct Intergroup Contact: The Potential Benefits of Acquaintance

C. Recategorization: Redrawing the Boundary between "Us" and "Them"

D. Cognitive Interventions: When Stereotypes Shatter—or at Least Become Less Compelling

IV. Prejudice Based on Gender: Its Nature and Effects

A. Gender Stereotypes: The Cognitive Core of Sexism

B. Discrimination against Females: Subtle but Often Deadly

    1. The role of expectations

    2. The role of confidence and self-perceptions

    3. Negative reactions to female leaders

    4. The "glass ceiling"—and above: Why women don't rise to the top

C. Sexual Harassment: When Discrimination Hits Rock Bottom

D. Beyond the Headlines: As Social Psychologists See it: Can a Lecture Be Sexually Harassing?

LEARNING OBJECTIVES: WHAT YOU SHOULD LEARN

As you are reading the chapter, these objectives provide page-by-page questions for you to answer. Answering the objectives should assure that you understand the essential material in the chapter.

1. Define "prejudice," "discrimination," and "schemas." Who takes longer to identify a racially ambiguous person, high or low prejudiced people? Explain how the Vanman group (1997) showed that facial muscles reveal the negative feelings generated by thoughts about targets of prejudice. Indicate how high and low prejudiced people's facial muscles reacted to photos of targets. [210-212]

2. Describe the role of prejudice in self-concept maintenance. Discuss Fein and Spencer's (1997) study which exploited JAP prejudice to reveal anti-Semitism among those who "failed" an I.Q. test. Indicate how putting down Jews affected the self-esteem of the "failed". [213-214]

3. How do stereotypes save cognitive energy? Indicate what has replaced blatant forms of discrimination. List the three components of "modern racism." What belief is modern racism associated with? Define "tokenism" and tell how "affirmative action hirees" are regarded. [214-215]

4. Indicate how tokens thrown to targets of prejudice are used as "proof" of "non-prejudice" and as a source of damage to the self-confidence of the targets. Define "reverse discrimination" and discuss how it may be both beneficial and detrimental to targets of prejudice. [215-217]

5. Describe how Harber (1998) showed that students subtly demonstrate reverse discrimination when grading black children's essays. Discuss the implications of a white student's reverse discrimination suit against the U. of Michigan. Define "realistic conflict" theory. Track the course of conflict escalation when "enemy" groups compete.[217-219]

6. Describe the Robbers cave study: the formation of rival groups, conflict between groups, results of conflict, and resolution involving "superordinate goals". Discuss how economic frustration led to inter-racial aggression in the first part of this century (Hovland and Sears, 1940). Relate "displaced aggression" to lynchings. Is "increased prejudice" a better explanation of lynchings? [219-222]

7. Describe the social learning view; define "social norms." Discuss how portrayals of minorities have recently changed. Indicate how "us" regards "them" and vice versa. Describe attributions by "in-group" to "outgroup" and to "in-group." [222-224]

8. Discuss the affective tone and level of generality of men's and women's attributions to each other. What does identifying with a group do for us? Describe the social identity theory expectation regarding our reactions to an out-group that is similar to "us" and threatening or not. [224]

9. Discuss how Henderson-King's et al's (1997) study of Russian students' reactions to former fellow Soviet members confirms social identity theory. What's a stereotype? Discuss possession of stereotypes about groups with whom we've had no contact. [225-226]

10. Discuss how stereotypes screen information for us, affect our information processing speed, and cause us to deal with information inconsistent with them. Define tacit inferences. Discuss the Dunning and Sherman (1997) study involving sentences consistent or inconsistent with activated stereotypes. Describe "inferential prisons." [226-227]

11. Describe the Whaley & Link (1998) study in which attributions were made to the homeless based on estimated percent who were people of color or just "male." Define "stereotype threat" (Steele, 1997). Discuss the Croizete and Claire (1998) study where low socioeconomic people were threatened with the "you're dumb" stereotype. [228-229]

12. Describe the Kawakami et al. (1998) study where high or low prejudiced people saw stereotype priming words and then had to mouth positive or negative stereotypes of blacks. Give a real life example of "illusory correlation." Do whites correctly estimate the black/white arrest rate? [229-230]

13. Indicate why rare behaviors performed by minority people are more cognitively accessible. Discuss the qualification of "distinctiveness based interpretation" and the contextual nature of prejudice. Discuss "out-group homogeneity" and "in-group differentiation". [230-232]

14. Discuss the accuracy of cross-racial identification. Are people born to be bigots? Indicate what parents can do about prejudice. Describe what bigotry does to the bigot. Discuss the "contact hypothesis". Know the conditions under which inter-group contact can lower prejudice. [232-235]

15. Why does the "extended" contact hypothesis works better than the original (Pettigrew, 1997)? Describe the Wright et al. (1997) study where knowledge of cross-group friendships changed. Define "recategorization" and the "common in-group identity model. [235-236]

16. Discuss how working together cooperatively can lead to recategorization. Contrast category-driven and attribute driven cognitive processing and indicate how the latter reduces prejudice. Discuss how "outcome based assessment" can be harnessed to fight stereotypes. [237-239]

17. Describe how Affirmation Action Programs (AAPs) may improve our perception of AAP hirees. Define sexism and indicate its status in the world today. Give some examples of gender stereotypes and consider their accuracy. Discuss reasons why progress of women has been slow. [239-241]

18. Indicate why women have lower expectations. Compare men and women on self-confidence. Describe Beyer's and Bowden's (1997) study that showed where women are self-confident. Indicate how subordinates react to women leaders, especially those with masculine traits. [241-242]

19. Describe the "glass ceiling". How does it hinder women's advancement? Discuss women's failure to get the tasks and be privy to the inside information leading to advancement. Discuss Lyness' and Thompson's findings (1997) on women's salary, promotion, etc. [242-243]

20. What kind of woman has penetrated the glass ceiling, and what is the downside of women's current status? Indicate three varieties of sexual harassment and its scope. What percent of women are harassed? [243-245]

21. Define sex role spillover and its implications for women in "masculine jobs". Discuss Burgess and Borgida (1997) where the genders rated the seriousness of sexual harassment (note: gender differences as a function of job type). Should a lecture implying hatred of men end up in civil court? [245-247]

There's More Than First Meets Your Eyes: Understanding Figures in Your Text

Turn to the figures in your text that are mentioned below and follow the discussion about how the figures can increase you understanding of research and theory.

1. Figure 6.2 (p. 212) provides insight into the nature of "reverse discrimination". These presumably liberal white student participants expressed more positive attitudes toward blacks than whites on a questionnaire. But those positive expressions may been made to maintain self-perceptions of fairmindedness. Their underlying negative feelings about blacks (black bars below the horizontal line) suggest that their questionnaire responses were made to compensate for negative expressions made under other circumstances.

2. Figure 6.6 (p. 217), like figure 6.2, may say something important about "reverse discrimination". White participants may be compensating for negative expressions about blacks made under different circumstances by favoring blacks in essay writing. If they are worried about being seen as "racist", because of negative reactions in other circumstances, they can "balance the scales" with their overly favorable essay grading. With the scales thus balanced, they can maintain a "fairmindeded" self-concept. Notice they choose the more ambiguous "content" as the arena for the "reverse discrimination". Remember also that this bogus grading may be more harmful to black students than helpful. While it might provide a temporary self-esteem boost unsupported by real accomplishment, it would avoid teaching them writing.

3. Figure 6.8 (p. 222) and the accompanying text shows important trends: while lynching went down over time, it rose in bad economic times, relative to good times occurring in closely adjacent years.

4. Figure 6.11 (p. 228) neatly shows the cognitive gymnastics humans are able to perform in order to transform information that weakens stereotypes into information that strengthens them.

5. Look at Figure 6.12 (p. 230) and the accompanying text. Even though previous research has revealed that even whites who score low on a prejudice test show subtle signs that racism influences them, research has consistently shown that whites who score high on a prejudice test show more negative affect directed to blacks than low scorers. This study reflects that difference. High prejudiced participants primed with "black" reacted more quickly to words relating to stereotypes of blacks, than when primed with "white" and exposed to other words.

6. Look at Figure 6.15 (p. 236) and the accompanying text. First, it is evident that competition generates prejudice relative to cooperation (middle bar compared to rightmost and leftmost bars). Second, friendship (right-most bar) is even better than team building (left-most bar) for lowering prejudice.

KEY TERMS: CONCEPTS YOU NEED TO UNDERSTAND

Write out the meaning of the following terms in your own words. Cover the right-hand portion of the exercise until you have finished, then check on the accuracy of your answers by comparing them with the definitions provided.

1.	modern racism	denial that discrimination continues, antagonism to the demands of minorities, and resentment of "special favors given to" minorities [215]
2.	stereotype	belief that all members of a group have certain characteristics and behave in certain ways [226]
3.	illusory correlation	a tendency to overestimate the rate of negative behaviors in small groups. [230]
4.	prejudice	refers to a special type of attitude—generally, a negative one—toward the members of some social group [211]
5.	sexism	prejudice based on gender [239]
6.	sexual harassment	defined in the U.S. as unwelcome sexual advances, requests for sexual favors, and other verbal or physical conduct of a sexual nature [244]

MATCHING:

Match each concept on the left side of the next page with an identifying phrase, word, or sentence on the right side of the page. The answers may be found after the WHAT'S WRONG HERE? section.

A.	ultimate attribution error	__ 1.	extended contact hypothesis
B.	down side of tokenism	__ 2.	"they're all alike"
C.	favoring other group more than own group	__ 3.	equal status
D.	the out-group is seen as homogeneous	__ 4.	reverse discrimination
E.	merely knowing that own group members have other group friends	__ 5.	attributional favoritism toward one's own group ("us"; ingroup)
F.	when intergroup contact works	__ 6.	targets not treated well by colleagues
G.	Explains the "glass ceiling"	__ 7.	women's lack of developmental opportunities: important tasks and inside information

WHAT'S WRONG HERE?

For each statement below indicate what needs to be changed in order to make the statement correct. You will find the answers at the end of the exercise, along with pages in the text where you can find more information.

1. The boys in Sherif's Robber's Cave study experienced friendly interaction throughout the experiment.

2. Outgroup homogeneity—seeing members of the other group as all alike—is the same as ingroup differentiation.

3. Learning of a stereotype target's success will tend to promote the stereotype.

4. Dunning's and Sherman's (1997) participants reported having seen more stereotype inconsistent sentences than consistent sentences.

5. Stereotypes are "inferential prisons" because once they form they restrict collection of stereotype confirming information.

6. Discrimination refers to actions directed toward a target, regardless of whether the behavior in question is positive or negative.

7. Hovland and Sears (1940) found that good economic times increased lynching, because whites became threatened by loss of success to blacks.

8. High distinctiveness" of a group and its behavior upon the first encounter with the group seems necessary for the development of the "illusory correlation".

9. If an out-group is seen as similar to one's in-group, that out-group will be regarded more favorably.

10. An advantage of intergroup contact lies in the possibility that members of the groups interacting will see similarities to themselves among members of the "other" group.

11. Gaertner and colleagues regard "recategorization" as the tendency of cooperative groups to re-erect the "us-them" boundaries between them once those boundaries are broken down.

12. Harasty (1997) found that when people make negative attributions to an out-group, they tend to qualify them: "Most men are messy."

13. Tajfel and colleagues argue that identifying with a social group has many benefits, but raising self-esteem is not one of them.

14. Following Steele's (1997) lead, Croizete and Claire (1998) found that low socioeconomic people threatened with the stereotype that they are low in intelligence received a boost in motivation and performed better than if not threatened.

MATCHING ANSWERS

5-A [224]; 6-B [214-216]; 4-C [216]; 2-D [224]; 1-E [235]; 3-F [234]; 7-G [243]

WHAT'S WRONG HERE? ANSWERS

1. Not so. The competition (realistic conflict theory) that came later was the source of strife between groups. [219-220]
2. No, it is the opposite. [231-232]
3. No; it will counter the stereotype. [239]
4. Not the case. They reported seeing more consistent than inconsistent sentences. [227]
5. Make that "stereotype disconfirming information". [227]
6. Not quite. Discrimination is behavior, but it is typically thought of as negative. [214]
7. Not so. Lynching increases in bad times, possibly because of displaced aggression or increased prejudice. [221-222]
8. No, high distinctiveness can develop after the first encounter. [230-231]
9. Not entirely true; it is true only if the out-group is not seen as a threat (Henderson-King et al., 1997). [225-226]
10. True, but perceived similarity does not always lead to decreased prejudice. [234-235]
11. False; cooperating groups break down boundaries. [237]
12. No, instead they made very global/universal attributions. [224]
13. No, the Tajfel group argue that people bolster their self-esteem by identifying with a social group. [224]
14. No, as expected based on Steele's theory, when threatened by sensitizing them to a negative stereotype about them, they performed worse. [229]

TRUE-FALSE

Indicate whether each of the following statements is true or false. If false, indicate why. Correct answers are found at the end of the exercise.

1. While blatant forms of prejudice and discrimination seem to have declined, racism may have just gone underground (become a bit more subtle).

2. The rival groups in the Robber's Cave study came together in harmony by the end of the study after they had undergone group therapy.

3. We identify with groups to enhance our self-esteem, as confirmed by Fein and Spencer (1997) whose participants failed an I.Q. test or not then rated a "Jew" or an "Italian".

4. Whaley and Link (1992) found that the higher the percentage of homeless estimated to be black, the stronger would negative stereotypes of blacks be activated and the more the homeless would be seen as lazy and dangerous.

5. As Minard showed in 1952, the more black and white miners failed to interact outside the mine, the more the failed to interact inside the mine.

6. Whites but not blacks identify their own race with greater accuracy than the other race.

7. A schema is a cognitive framework for organizing, interpreting and recalling information.

8. Media portrayal of blacks, which improved during the 60s, 70s, and 80s, are getting more negative in the 90s.

9. According learning view, children learn negative attitudes toward various groups from their parents.

10. Social norms are rules of a given group suggesting what actions or attitudes are appropriate.

11. About 10% of women indicate that they have been sexually harassed.

12. Category driven and attribute driven processing refer to focusing on, unique characteristics and group membership respectively.

13. Affirmation action can be beneficial by improving the outcomes of women and people of color.

14. Part of women's advancement problem is that they tend to have lower expectations and self-confidence, but this problem should not be over-emphasized: women don't lack self-confidence on feminine tasks (Beyer & Bowden, 1997).

15. Women leaders are considered exceptions and get "exception treatment": they receive high evaluations, and are targeted for positive non-verbal behaviors, especially by men.

TRUE-FALSE ANSWERS

1. True. [214-215]
2. False; they ended hostilities after pursuing a superordinate goal together. [219-226]
3. True. [213]
4. True. [228]
5. False; prejudice can be situational: blacks and whites interacted well in the mine but basically not at all outside it. [231]
6. False; both misidentify the other race, but blacks do so with less inaccuracy [232]
7. True. [211]
8. False; they are getting better. [222-223]
9. True. [222]
10. True. [222]
11. False; triple that figure and then some. [244]
12. False; reverse "unique characteristics" and "group membership". [238]
13. True. [239]
14. True [241]
15. False; women leaders are targeted for negative non-verbal behavior and receive low evaluations, especially if they show masculine behavior. [242]

FILL IN THE BLANKS: A GUIDED REVIEW

Mentally fill in each of the blanks in the following section while covering the answers in the margin. Check each answer against the answer in the margin by uncovering as you go along.

1. Infrequent events may stand out in memory because they are _____.

   distinctive [230-231]

2. "Passive," "dependent", "gossipy", "emotional" are negative stereotypes of ____, but they exaggerate gender _____.

   women; differences [240]

3. Sexual harassment can be described as attention that is _____ and is _____ in nature.

   unwanted; sexual [244-245]

4. Lyness and Thompson (1977) report that high ____ women did well in a study involving a large company and matching of the genders on relevant factors, despite having fewer _____ confronting more ____ and having more ___ ____.

   competent; subordinates; obstacles; interruptions [243-244]

5. ___ ___ occurs when women hold jobs with mostly male employees. When women are __ ____ by holding non-traditional jobs, they experience more ___ __ and tended to see it as more ___ than men did.

   Sex role spillover; role deviates; sexual harassment; severe [245-246]

6. The "they all look alike" effect appears to be stronger for _____ than for _____ _____.

   European Americans; African Americans [232]

7. _____ _____ allowed the resolution of hostilities among the groups in the Robber's Cave study, but the study was limited because the subjects were all _____ from _____ backgrounds.

   superordinate goals; boys; homogeneous [220]

MULTIPLE–CHOICE QUESTIONS: A PERSONAL QUIZ

After you have finished reading the chapter and done the other exercises in the STUDY GUIDE, take the quiz found below to test your knowledge. Indicate your answers by circling the letter of the chosen alternative. Check your answers against the answers provided at the end of the exercise.

1. Prejudice refers to
   a. any kind of bias or inclination toward anything or anyone that may be considered inherently irrational.
   b. positive attitudes of a special kind.
   c. a usually negative attitude toward the members of some social group.
   d. attitudes of majority toward minority only.

2. In the famous "Robbers Cave" study by Sherif and colleagues
   a. interactions between groups were hostile from the beginning.
   b. boxing matches forced on the boys by the experimenters generated antagonism between groups.
   c. the boys began early to identify with their groups, even creating group flags.
   d. the boys had trouble developing group identities, until the experimenters assigned group names to them.

3. In the "us vs. them" orientation,
    a. "us" are viewed in highly favorable terms.
    b. "them" are viewed in neutral terms.
    c. "us" and "them" are seen as complementary rather than antagonistic.
    d. "us" and "them" are seen as merely dissimilar, not antagonistic.

4. Prejudice serves to
    a. work off one's hostilities
    b. harm the target but does good for the bigot
    c. promote "survival of the fittest"
    d. bolster prejudice people's self-images

5. What lies behind the "illusory correlation?"
    a. nothing but bigotry
    b. a well known brain mechanism
    c. the fact that infrequent events are distinctive
    d. a complex interaction between child rearing practices and cultural norms

6. Gaertner and colleagues' recategorization
    a. refers to a technique for collapsing the boundaries between antagonistic groups by having them pursue common goals.
    b. is a way to have groups switch identities.
    c. has been basically shown to be invalid by a number of studies.
    d. amounts to having prejudiced persons reclassify themselves as unprejudiced.

7. Why does contact between groups work to reduce prejudice?
    a. Contact may increase the perception of similarity of members belonging to the different groups.
    b. "Mere exposure" leads to liking regardless of circumstances.
    c. Contact promotes the illusion that groups are all alike.
    d. It works but nobody knows why.

8. Was a Lesbian college lecturer's implicit condemnation of men a good basis for a male student's law suit?
    a. yes, discrimination is discrimination
    b. no, freedom of speech takes precedence over everything else
    c. yes, its about time men get the treatment in class that women have been getting forever
    d. it is uncertain, the case was pending at the time this book went to press

9. Dollard and colleagues (1939) frustration and aggression theory predicted
    a. blacks would harbor much aggression against whites
    b. the lynching of blacks by whites during the earlier part of the 20th century
    c. that the civil rights movement would eventually succeed
    d. the out-pouring of sympathy for blacks on the part of liberal whites

10. How do people handle information that is inconsistent with a stereotype they hold?
    a. They assimilate it, and it changes their stereotype.
    b. They show a boomerang effect; it makes their stereotype much stronger.
    c. They deny it or refute it.
    d. They misconstrue it as supporting their stereotype.

11. According to the social learning point of view, negative attitudes toward various social groups are due to
    a. sex role training.
    b. inborn social tendencies.
    c. parents and friends.
    d. the political-economic-social climate.

12. Relative to men, women tend to be
    a. more ambitious.
    b. more concerned about money.
    c. less creative.
    d. less confident.

13. Pettigrew (1997 work regarding cross-group friendships revealed
    a. no relationship between cross-group friendships and other variables
    b. the greater the number of cross-group friendships, the more neutral the cross-group attitudes
    c. cross group friendships declined with the amount of time groups interacted
    d. the greater the number of cross-group friendships, the lower the inter-group prejudice

14. Only one of the following falls under "sexual harassment." Which one could be sexual harassment?
    a. A wife is seen being kissed by her husband on the job.
    b. A boss and a subordinate willingly have an affair.
    c. A boss repeatedly makes derogatory statements about women in front of women employees.
    d. A man consents to intercourse with a female boss.

15. Tokenism refers to
    a. refusing to accept even a token gesture of friendship from an object of prejudice.
    b. being merely occasionally unfriendly to objects of prejudice.
    c. passing out "tokens"—small rewards or praise—to other people who are unwilling to display discrimination.
    d. hiring a person solely as a token member of a racial or ethnic group, rather than on the basis of qualifications.

16. Reverse discrimination refers to
    a. the worse kind of discrimination.
    b. the most open kind of discrimination.
    c. bending over backwards to treat members of some social group favorably.
    d. trying to hide favorability toward some group by discriminating against its members.

17. Regarding the "glass ceiling;"
    a. male executives consciously erect it.
    b. it is a myth disproved by research.
    c. male executives unconsciously promote it.
    d. it was a problem, but has been solved by affirmative action.

18. Prejudice people are
    a. fortunately rare
    b. made not born
    c. the vast majority of people
    d. more blatant in their expressions than they used to be

MULTIPLE CHOICE ANSWERS

1. c [211]	6. a [237]	11. c [222]	16. c [216-217]
2. c [220]	7. a [234]	12. d [242]	17. c [242-243]
3. a [223-224]	8. d [247]	13. d [235]	18. b [233-234]
4. d [224]	9. b [221]	14. c [244-245]	
5. c [231]	10. c [227-8]	15. d [215-218]	

IF YOU'D LIKE TO KNOW MORE: FURTHER SOURCES OF INFORMATION

Toch, T. & Davis, J. (1990, April 23). Separate But Equal All Over Again. U.S. NEWS AND WORLD REPORT, 37-38. Deja vu. Even in 1990, Louisiana still has not desegregated its colleges and universities. Their case shows that segregation is still very much alive and well.

McLeod, B. (1986, July). The Oriental Express. PSYCHOLOGY TODAY, 48-52. Asian-Americans are the fastest growing minority. They are also highly successful. Obviously these two facts don't make a popular combination.

Trotter, R. J. (1985, Sept.). Muzafer Sherif: A Life of Conflict and Goals. PSYCHOLOGY, 55-59. Sherif talks about conflict resolution, starting with conflicts in his own life and including consideration of the famous summer camp study.

Vachss, A. (1993, June 27). Rapists are Single-Minded Sociopathic Beasts that Cannot Be Tamed with Understanding. PARADE, 4-6. In no instance is bias against women more devastating than in court where women rape victims are the focus of attention, not the accused rapist.

Nordland, R. (1996, Nov. 6). The Crimes of Bosnia. NEWSWEEK, 55. The nth degree of racism is seen in what the Nazis did in their infamous camps, and what the "ethnic cleansing" Bosnian Serbs allegedly did recently. Will the U.N. look the other way, or once and for all time say no to such racist acts by prosecuting the perpetrators?

Klein, J. (1996, Nov. 20). Heartbreaker. NEWSWEEK, 37-41. Why did Colin Powell, the first African-American with a real chance to become President of the U.S., decide not to run? Does it have anything to do with the times—soon after the Rodney King case and the O.J. trial widened the rift between European-Americans and African-Americans.

ASSOCIATED PRESS. Nov. 23, 1998 (St. Louis Post Dispatch, p.1). Religious bigotry has historically provided justification for numerous atrocities. In a recent example, Indonesian Muslim youths killed 6 during anti-Christian rioting. "In one attack Muslim mobs broke into a Roman Catholic church ... [during a wedding], shattering stained glass windows, chalices, and a statue of the Virgin Mary." Of course history includes violence going the other way.

http://www.webcom/~intvoice/ This site will allow you to connect to African-American sites, sites for people of "mixed race", and American Indian sites.

http://www.cnet.com/content/features/Net/Rainbow Multiculturalism is all about appreciating differences among people (and similarities!). Thus, it's all about getting along.

http://glaad.org/ Here is a site that addresses the last stand for bigots. People who wouldn't think of being anti-any ethnic group feel comfortable about being anti-gay. You can start here to help stop discrimination on the basis of sexual orientation.

THINKING CRITICALLY ABOUT PREJUDICE

1. There are rather few Lithuanians in the U.S. Their descendants are from a country that borders on Russia. Lithuania was a part of the old Soviet Union, but is now independent. On a 10 point scale, with 10 being "most criminal" and one being "least criminal," rate the degree to which Lithuanians show criminal behavior under two different conditions. First just rate them. Then rate them under the assumptions that underlie the "illusory correlation" effect. Are the two ratings different? If so, why?

2. What can parents do to lessen the likelihood that their children will be prejudiced? First have them look at themselves. What can they do about their own behavior, beliefs, and feeling? Second, have them look at their children's peers. This is a tougher problem. What can parents do to lessen the likelihood that prejudice will spread from their children's peers to their children? Finally, have them look at the media. What can parents do to prevent their children from picking up information in the media that will nourish prejudice?

3. The glass ceiling is an interesting phenomenon. Make a list of groups whose members are likely to be confronted with the glass ceiling. Add to the list some groups whose members are not likely to be faced with the glass ceiling. Now rank the groups from #1 (most likely to be confronted with the glass ceiling) to #[whatever the total number of your groups happens to be], the group least likely to be subject to the glass ceiling. For the most likely group (#1) indicate how they may be able to crack the glass ceiling. For the least likely group, indicate circumstances or situations in which they may have to face the glass ceiling.

4. Reverse discrimination is strange. It involves cases whereby people actually favor groups other than their own or groups that are normally discriminated against. Who is likely to show this kind of discrimination, high or low prejudiced persons? Whatever your choice, explain why those you chose resort to reverse discrimination. What are the "real" reasons for their reverse discrimination? Another way to put it is "What's in it for them?"

5. Can you think of a way that a stereotype might be born through the operation of the attribution process? Imagine a four-year-old boy who has yet to learn gender stereotypes. On an occasion, he witnesses a girl acting passively. Someone is telling her what to do and she is complying completely. 1) What attribution is likely to be directed toward her? 2) given that attribution, what is the boy likely to conclude the next time he witnesses a girl acting passively?

INTERPERSONAL ATTRACTION: INITIAL CONTACT, LIKING, BECOMING ACQUAINTED

CHAPTER OUTLINE: GETTING THE OVERALL PICTURE:

Before reading the chapter, it may be helpful to examine the chapter outline. This will give you an idea of what is covered in the chapter and should help you organize your learning and review the material. You can also record notes on text sections under the outline headings for those sections.

I. Recognizing and Evaluating Strangers: Proximity and Emotions

   A. Attraction: An Overview

      1. Attitudes about a Person

      2. Affect as the Basic Factor underlying Attraction

   B. Repeated Unplanned Contacts Lead to Attraction

   C. Beyond the Headlines: As Social Psychologists See It—Can Classroom Seating Assignments Affect One's Life?

   D. Affective State: Positive versus Negative Emotions as the Basis for Attraction

      1. Direct Effects of Affective State: Attraction toward a Person Who Arouses your Positive or Negative Feelings

      2. Indirect Effects of Affective State: Attraction toward a Person on the Basis of Independently Aroused Feelings

      3. What if There Are Multiple Sources of Affect and We Are Not Aware of Why We Feel as We Do?

      4. Just How Vulnerable Are We to Affective Manipulations?

II. Becoming Acquaintances: The Need to Affiliate and the Effect of Observable Characteristics

    A. Affiliation Need: Dispositional and Situational Determinants of Interpersonal Associations

        1. Individual Differences in the Need to Affiliate

        2. Situational Determinants of the Need to Affiliate

    B. Cornerstones of Social Psychology: Festinger's Social Comparison Theory

    C. Responding to Observable Characteristics: Instant Cues to Attraction

        1. Physical Attractiveness: Judging People as well as Books by their Covers

        2. What, Exatly, Do We Mean by Attractive?

        3. The Situation Can Influence Perceived Attractiveness

        4. Other Aspects of Appearance: Physique and Weight

        5. Other Aspects of Appearance and Behavior that Influence Attraction

III. Becoming Close Acquaintances and Moving toward Friendship: Similarity and Reciprocal Positive Evaluations

    A. Opposites Don't Attract, but Birds of a Feather Really Do Flock Together

        1. Attitude Similarity as a Determinant of Attraction

        2. Is Attraction Influenced by Similarity, Dissimilarity, or Both?

        3. Why Do Similar and Dissimilar Attitudes Influence Attraction?

        4. The Matching Hypothesis: Liking Those Who Are Most Like You

    B. Social Diversity: A Critical Analysis—Heterosexual Interracial Dating among Asian Americans

    C. Reciprocal Positive Evaluations: If You Like Me, I Like You

        1. Attraction: The Bigger Picture

LEARNING OBJECTIVES: WHAT YOU SHOULD LEARN

As you are reading the chapter, these objectives provide page-by-page questions for you to answer. Answering the objectives should assure that you understand the essential material in the chapter.

1. Define interpersonal attraction and summarize factors that lead us to be liked by some individuals and disliked by others. [255-257]

2. Describe the usual effect of repeated unplanned contacts on interpersonal attraction, along with why this happens and circumstances under which the effect fails to occur. [257-260]

3. Describe how classroom and residential proximity affects friendship formation and indicate how researchers have reached the conclusion that proximity <u>causes</u> attraction to occur. [260-263]

4. Summarize research demonstrating that when a person does something arousing positive or negative affect, he or she is liked or disliked accordingly. [263-264]

5. Summarize research demonstrating that when a person is simply associated with positive or negative affect, he or she is liked or disliked accordingly. [264-266]

6. Explain how participants' evaluations of Chinese characters were affected when exposures to the characters were accompanied by subliminal presentations of happy or angry faces. [266-267]

7. Describe how positive vs. negative affect influenced ratings given candidates by the least informed research participants. How did affect influence ratings given by the well-informed participants? [267-269]

8. Describe the need for affiliation as a trait, comparing explicit and implicit affiliation needs, and be familiar with Hill's four motives underlying affiliation. [270-271]

9. Give examples of situations that produce a need to affiliate, and explain why a patient awaiting coronary-bypass surgery is best off when his roommate already had the same surgery. [271-273]

10. Understand how we evaluate our opinions and abilities according to Festinger's social comparison theory. [274-275]

11. Describe how physical attractiveness is related to opposite-sex attraction and perceived desirability as a reproductive partner. [276-277]

12. Why are men more influenced by the physical attractiveness of a potential partner, whereas women are more influenced by maturity, education level, etc.? [277]

13. Describe the stereotypes we hold of attractive and less attractive individuals and indicate how these stereotypes affect interpersonal judgments. [277-279]

14. Describe how adults respond to attractive babies, and also describe how babies respond differently to attractive vs. less attractive adults. [279-280]

15. Describe appearance anxiety in women and note negative qualities associated with good looks. [280]

16. Contrast the finding that males rate females with either "childlike" or "mature" features to be attractive with the finding that "average" faces are attractive. [280-282]

17. Describe the "contrast effect" in physical attractiveness ratings, along with the effect of a fast-approaching closing time. [282-283]

18. Examine stereotypes that exist for endomorphs, mesomorphs, and ectomorphs, and examine the negative stereotypes that exist for overweight persons. [283-285]

19. Summarize the "other aspects of appearance and behavior" that influence how we are perceived by others. [286-287]

20. How have researchers documented the idea that similar attitudes cause an increase in liking, rather than accepting some of the other logically-possible hypotheses? [288-289]

21. Understand the fact that the similarity-attraction effect seems to be based on the proportion of similar attitudes expressed, regardless of total number of topics. [289-290]

22. Using Rosenbaum's repulsion hypothesis, explain the role of similar vs. dissimilar attitudes in creating the similarity-attraction effect. What is the text's basis for rejecting the repulsion hypothesis? How is the false consensus effect related to the repulsion hypothesis? [290-291]

23. Understand how each of the following explains the similarity-attraction effect: a) balance theory; b) social comparison theory; and c) Rushton's biological view. [291-292]

24. Describe evidence that supports the matching hypothesis, and indicate how we respond when couples are obviously mismatched in physical attractiveness. [292-293]

25. Discuss the effects of race and ethnicity on interpersonal choices for dates and marriage partners, and assess the factors leading to interracial attraction. [293-294]

26. How is our liking for someone affected when they flatter us or use other ingratiation tactics? [294-296]

There's More Than First Meets Your Eyes: Understanding Figures in Your Text

Turn to the figures in your text that are mentioned below and follow the discussion about how the figures can increase you understanding of research and theory.

1. Figure 7.1 (page 256) seems to conceptualize the level of attraction as varying on a 5-point Likert scale, where 1=strong liking, 2=mild liking, 3=neither liking nor disliking, 4=mild disliking, and 5=strong disliking. Note the types of interaction expected from persons whose attraction level falls at the various levels.

2. Figure 7.7 (page 265) describes the fact that positive or negative feelings can be conceptualized as the intervening event between stimulus conditions we encounter and our ultimate attraction toward the stimulus. The direct effect presented in the top half of each figure is so obvious that it can be misunderstood. The delicious chocolate cake causes positive feelings and that's why I like the cake. The indirect effect is not so intuitively obvious. Any stimulus simply associated with the cake becomes associated with the positive feelings aroused by the cake. Thus neutral stimuli can become liked merely by being associated with any stimulus arousing positive feelings.

3. Figure 7.9 (page 269) talks about a study that tried to apply the theory presented in Figure 7.7. Some people were made to experience positive feelings ("a positive mood"), whereas others were made to experience negative feelings ("a negative mood"). Any stimulus encountered while feeling good should be evaluated positively, while any stimulus encountered while feeling bad should be evaluated negatively. Ottati and Isbell found the expected result when students encountered a heretofore unknown stimulus person. But when students encountered a stimulus person they already knew much about, current mood wasn't simply transferred to the stimulus person in the expected way.

4. Figure 7.13 (page 279) shows that even one-year-olds respond more positively to an attractive adult than to an unattractive adult stranger.

5. Figure 7.14 (page 281) shows how a computer can be used to create a face that is the "average" of two faces. Faces created by this averaging process are generally rated as more attractive than either of the original faces.

6. Figure 7.15 (page 283) shows that when we're in the presence of photographs of very attractive models, we tend to rate ourselves more negatively than when no photographs are present.

7. The affect-centered model of attraction presented in Figure 7.20 (page 296) basically repeats the same idea previously presented in Figure 7.7 (see number 2 above). In Figure 7.7 the "neutral stimulus" was described quite generically. In Figure 7.20 it is assumed that the neutral stimulus is another person. Whatever affective response is aroused becomes associated with the person and our evaluation and behavior toward them is a function of our affect.

KEY TERMS: CONCEPTS YOU NEED TO UNDERSTAND

Write out the meaning of the following terms in your own words. Cover the right-hand portion of the exercise until you have finished, then check on the accuracy of your answers by comparing them with the definitions provided.

1.	interpersonal attraction	the evaluation we make of other individuals; this attitudinal dimension ranges from strong dislike at one extreme to strong liking at the other [256]
2.	proximity	environmentally-determined physical distance between people; close proximity increases the likelihood of interaction and of friendship [258]
3.	need for social comparaison	refers to uor tendency to evaluate our opinions and abilities by comparing them to opinions and abilities of others, especially similar others [274-275]
4.	indirect effect of an affective state	to respond evaluatively to someone who is associated with an emotion we experience even though the emotion was created by something else [265-266]
5.	matching hypothesis	proposal stating that people who are similar or who have similar social assets will select each others as friends, lovers, etc. [292]
6.	repulsion hypothesis	Rosenbaum's discredited proposal that attitude similarity does not increase attraction, but instead that attitude dissimilarity decreases attraction [290]
7.	balance theory	theory which explains the similarity effect by noting that we prefer balanced relationships and find imbalanced and non balanced relationships to be less pleasant [291]
8.	reciprocal positive evaluations	our tendency to like others when they express liking for us [294]
9.	the affect-centered model of attraction	says that whether we like or dislike someone depends on how we feel when we encounter him/her; if we feel good, this good feeling becomes assocaited with the encountered person [296]

MATCHING:

Match each concept on the left with an identifying phrase, word or sentence on the right. The answers follow the **WHAT'S WRONG HERE?** section.

A.	entails close proximity	__	1.	one of Hill's affiliative needs
B.	social support	__	2.	muscular body type
C.	cute/flippant opening line	__	3.	"men seek reproductive success"
D.	endomorph	__	4.	sitting near someone
E.	mesomorph	__	5.	round, fat body type
F.	ectomorph	__	6.	user is not very well liked
G.	evolutionary theory	__	7.	thin, angular body type
H.	similar other person	__	8.	preferred for social comparison

WHAT'S WRONG HERE?

For each statement below indicate what needs to be changed in order to make the statement correct. You will find the answers at the end of the exercise, along with pages in the text where you can find more information.

1. Repeated exposure generally has the effect of decreasing our liking for a stimulus.

2. Infants are more likely to smile at a photograph of someone they've never seen before than of someone they have seen previously.

3. In order for exposure to produce liking, the exposure(s) must be for a long enough time period so that the person is aware of the exposure.

4. The effect of repeated exposure is so powerful that repeated exposure to someone who initially evokes extremely negative feelings produces liking.

5. Students who simply sit side-by-side in a classroom are not likely to become friends.

6. When researchers studied people's reactions to a laundered shirt, they found the quality of the shirt was the only factor that determined how it was rated.

7. When a person with a stigma such as obesity interacts with someone else, the second person will probably not acquire any of the negative affect associated with the stigma.

8. The four basic motives proposed by Hill (1987) to underlie the disposition to be affiliative are positive stimulation, social support, social comparison, and intimacy.

9. In the classic Schachter (1959) studies, subjects expecting to receive painful electric shocks preferred waiting alone rather than with other subjects.

10. The mechanism operating to produce increased affiliation in response to fear seems to be higher-order conditioning.

11. Research comparing behavior and personality characteristics of attractive and less attractive persons have found no actual characteristics on which attractive and less attractive persons differ.

12. Men demonstrate just as much appearance anxiety as women.

13. There is little agreement among people as to who is attractive and who is not attractive.

14. There are no specific characteristics that researchers have been able to document that cause viewers to perceive that a female is attractive.

15. According to studies examining computer-generated faces, attractive people generally possess facial characteristics that deviate in some way from average.

MATCHING ANSWERS:

1–B [271]; 2–E [283]; 3–G [277]; 4–A [258]; 5–D [283]; 6–C [264]; 7–F [283]; 8–H [274]

WHAT'S WRONG HERE? ANSWERS:

1. Generally, repeated exposure *increases* our liking. [258-259]
2. Familiarity causes an increase in smiling. [258]
3. Even exposures so brief that subjects are not aware of the exposures produce the exposure effect; in fact, subliminal exposures have a bigger than usual impact. [259-260]
4. Repeated exposure alone is not sufficient to overcome strong initial dislike. [260]
5. Proximity *is* generally sufficient to produce liking. [260-262]
6. Shirts that had been worn by a liked person were given more positive ratings. [266]
7. The negative affect aroused by the stigmatized person's "condition" is often transferred to the other person. [266]
8. Intimacy is *not* one of Hill's motives. Instead, the fourth motive is attention. [271]
9. Subjects expecting shocks preferred waiting together with others. [272]
10. The mechanism seems to be a need for social comparison so subjects can evaluate their perceptions and emotional reactions. [272]
11. Though differences are not as great as stereotypes suggest, attractive persons have been shown to possess greater social skills and to be more popular. [278-279]
12. Women seem to worry more about their appearance than men do. [280]
13. While people find it difficult to identify the precise cues that determine physical attractiveness, they agree as to who is attractive. [280]
14. Cunningham (1986) found two distinct types of faces that were rated attractive. One group had "childlike features" and the other had "mature" features. [280]
15. In fact, a computer-generated "average" face is generally attractive. [281]

TRUE–FALSE:

Indicate whether each of the following statements is true or false. If false, indicate why. Correct answers are found at the end of the exercise.

1. The idea that proximity leads to attraction is just as well documented by correlational studies as by experimental studies.

2. When another person is simply present when your feelings happen to be positive or negative (for some reason unrelated to that person), you still tend to evaluate him or her based on your own affective state.

3. When asked to rate males shown in photographs, female subjects rated the photographed individuals more positively if there was music playing in the background.

4. When a subject hears good news just before encountering a stranger, the stranger is liked more than if bad news is heard.

5. While subjects tend to stigmatize a man on the basis of his being gay, there is no negative reaction carried over to someone who is a heterosexual friend of that person.

6. Infants do not respond any differently to an attractive stranger than to an unattractive stranger.

7. As closing time approached in a college bar, researchers found members of the opposite sex were rated to be less attractive.

8. The somatotype which is viewed most positively is the endomorph.

9. When subjects judged underweight, average weight, and overweight somatotypes, the most negative ratings were given the overweight individual.

10. If shown a someone's picture and given no information about his opinions, we tend to attribute to him attitudes different from our own.

11. Research has found that pairs of same-sex friends and pairs of opposite-sex friends are more similar in attractiveness than randomly-matched pairs.

12. We like people who evaluate us positively even if the evaluation is inaccurate or an attempt at flattery.

13. Outdating and interracial marriages have decreased in frequency over the last few decades.

14. The affect-centered model of attraction assumes that negative emotions aroused when we are simply in the presence of another person can lead us to evaluate that person negatively.

15. The best opening line for producing a positive reaction with an opposite-sex stranger is to use a straightforward, direct opening line.

TRUE-FALSE ANSWERS:

1. False; experimental studies manipulating proximity are methodologically stronger. [262]
2. True. [263]
3. False; background music increased liking only when it was *liked* music. [265-266]
4. True. [265-266]
5. False; not only is the gay man stigmatized, but so is his heterosexual friend. [266]
6. False; twelve-month-old infants responded more positively to an adult wearing an attractive mask than to an adult wearing an unattractive mask. [279]
7. False; as closing time approached, opposite-sex individuals were rated more attractive. [282-283]
8. False; endomorphs, who are round and fat, are viewed negatively. [283-284]
9. True [284-285]

10. False; in fact, we assume the person is similar to us, as predicted by the false consensus effect. [291]
11. True. [292]
12. True. [294]
13. False; there has been an increase in both. [293-294]
14. True. [296]
15. True. [264]

FILL IN THE BLANKS: A GUIDED REVIEW

Mentally fill in each of the blanks in the following section while covering the answers in the margin. Check each answer against the answer in the margin by uncovering as you go along.

1. The fact that friendships tend to develop between people who live near each other or work together demonstrates the effect of _____ on attraction.

   proximity [258]

2. Zajonc argued that repeated exposure leads to _____ in attraction.

   an increase [258]

3. The personality dimension that involves a need to spend time with people and to interact whenever possible is the _____.

   need for affiliation [270]

4. A researcher who assumes that individuals differ from one another in the degree to which they possess a need for affiliation is treating affiliation need as a _____.

   trait or disposition [270]

5. Psychologists who measure the need for affiliation by using questionnaires that ask subjects to report relevant desires and activities directly are measuring _____ motivation to affiliate.

   explicit [270]

6. Psychologists who measure the need to affiliate by analyzing stories subjects write in response to ambiguous pictures are measuring _____ motivation to affiliate.

   implicit [270]

7. When people affiliate out of a desire to elicit the praise and approval of others, their affiliation is based on a need for _____.

   attention [271]

8. When affiliation is based on a need to reduce uncomfortable feelings of uncertainty about what is going on, the affiliation is based on a need for _____.

   social comparison [271]

9. The idea that men emphasize female attractiveness because youth and vitality are associated with females' reproductive capacity is based on _____ theory.

   evolutionary [276-277]

10. The idea that women emphasize a male's ability to provide resources for her and her offspring rather than his physical attractiveness is based on _____ theory.

   evolutionary [276-277]

11. The proposal that attitude similarity has no effect on attraction, and that instead we dislike people who express dissimilar attitudes is known as the _____ hypothesis.

repulsion [290]

12. The false belief that "almost everyone agrees with me" is known as the _____ effect.

false consensus [291]

13. When two people like each other and agree, there is _____; when two people like one another and disagree, there is _____; when two people dislike each other, there is _____.

balance; imbalance; nonbalance [291]

14. The idea that we like those who evaluate us positively is known as the _____ effect.

reciprocal positive evaluations [294]

15. The proposal that positive or negative feelings, no matter how they are aroused, become associated with whatever person happens to be around at the moment is a central idea of the _____ model of attraction.

affect-centered [296]

MULTIPLE-CHOICE QUESTIONS: A PERSONAL QUIZ

After you have finished reading the chapter and done the other exercises in the STUDY GUIDE, take the quiz found below to test your knowledge. Indicate your answers by circling the letter of the chosen alternative. Check your answers against the answers provided at the end of the exercise.

1. Subliminal repeated exposure has been shown to
   a. produce no change in liking for the exposed stimulus.
   b. cause subjects to dislike the exposed stimulus.
   c. increase liking for the exposed stimulus.
   d. produce recognition of the exposed stimulus, but no change in liking.

2. Moreland and Beach (1992) had female assistants attend a college class not at all, a few times, or several times. When members of the class rated the assistant for likability, it was found that
   a. how often assistants attended class did not affect likability.
   b. assistants who attended a few times were rated more likeable.
   c. assistants who attended several times were rated more likeable.
   d. frequency of attendance was not important; the only significant factor was assistants' attractiveness.

3. Early studies that investigated the effect of location of residence on the likelihood couples will marry found that
   a. proximity had no impact.
   b. proximity was related to marriage, but social class and racial differences were the real causal factor.
   c. close proximity was negatively related to marriage.
   d. people tended to marry individuals who lived nearby.

4. Which of the following has been found in classroom studies?
   a. people seated at the end of a row make more friends than those seated in the middle.
   b. when seating is alphabetical, friendships seldom form with people whose names begin with the same or a nearby letter.
   c. someone seated to your right or left is not likely to become your friend.
   d. changing seat assignments once or twice a semester results in each student having more acquaintances.

5. What was the effect of having subjects listen to pleasant background music while they rated a stranger?
   a. The stranger was liked more.
   b. The stranger was liked less because he seemed negative when contrasted with the pleasant music.
   c. Hearing pleasant music did not, by itself, affect liking.
   d. Unless the music was specifically produced by the stranger, it produced no effect.

6. Ottati and Isbell (1996) studied the effects of mood on how people evaluated a political candidate. How did mood affect participants' evaluations of the candidate?
   a. People who were well-informed were most affected by their mood.
   b. People who were poorly-informed rated candidates positively no matter what their mood.
   c. People who were poorly-informed rated candidates positively when in a good mood and negatively when in a bad mood.
   d. People who were well-informed rated candidates positively when in a good mood and negatively when in a bad mood.

7. In the classic Schachter (1959) studies, subjects expecting to receive painful electric shocks
   a. preferred waiting with other subjects rather than being along.
   b. preferred waiting along rather than with other subjects.
   c. generally didn't care whether they waited together or alone.
   d. sneaked out the back door before the experiment began.

8. Which of the following is <u>not</u> one of the three basic assumptions underlying Festinger's theory of social comparison?
   a. If objective criteria are available, we use these to evaluate ourselves.
   b. Human beings have a basic drive to evaluate their opinions and abilities.
   c. When engaging in social comparison, we prefer making comparisons with persons similar to us.
   d. The first way we seek to evaluate ourselves is through social comparison.

9. Which of the following is consistent with evolutionary considerations among individuals seeking a romantic partner?
   a. Males seek a youthful partner because female youthfulness is a sign of fertility.
   b. Females seek a youthful partner because male youthfulness is a sign of fertility.
   c. Females seek a partner who has the ability to provide resources for their children.
   d. both a and c

10. With regard to the effect of attractiveness on preferences, it has been shown that
    a. one-year olds respond equally to an adult wearing an attractive or an unattractive mask.
    b. one-year olds respond more positively to an adult wearing the attractive mask.
    c. one-year olds respond more positively to an adult wearing the unattractive mask.
    d. adults are affected by the attractiveness of a one-year old, but one-year olds are not affected by attractiveness.

11. Which of the following has(have) been found by research to be attractive features in a face?
    a. "childlike" features in women
    b. "mature" features in women
    c. an "average" face created by digitizing
    d. all of the above

12. The study which distorted video images in order to examine perceptions of persons with various somatotypes suggested that _____ are perceived differently than the other two types.
    a. ectomorphs
    b. mesomorphs
    c. endomorphs
    d. none of the above

13. Which of the following is true?
    a. Studies have shown that the number of shared attitudes is important in determining liking, but not the proportion of shared attitudes.
    b. Research finds that people who like each other are no more similar in attitudes than randomly matched pairs.
    c. There is little support for the similarity-attraction hypothesis in areas outside attitude similarity.
    d. Our tendency to like others who agree with us was demonstrated in the study of transfer students who shared a housing unit.

14. Rosenbaum's repulsion hypothesis states that
    a. we respond to handicapped persons with stigmatizing prejudice.
    b. we respond to physically unattractive individuals with rejection.
    c. when couples are mismatched for physical attractiveness, we expect their relationship to be unstable.
    d. our liking for a stranger shifts negatively when the stranger expresses dissimilar attitudes.

15. When two people like each other and agree, there is _____; when two people like one another and disagree, there is _____; when two people dislike one another, there is _____.
    a. balance; imbalance; nonbalance
    b. balance; nonbalance; imbalance
    c. nonbalance; imbalance; balance
    d. imbalance; nonbalance; balance

16. The tendency for people to choose as partners persons who possess attributes similar to their own is known as the _____ hypothesis.
    a. matching
    b. equity
    c. need compatibility
    d. complementarity

17. What did Fujino (1997) find to be the strongest predictor of whether an Asian student would date someone of another race?
    a. the degree to which he/she had adopted aspects of American culture
    b. acculturation
    c. physical attractiveness
    d. proximity

18. When people believe another person likes them, they tend to like the other person. The term that describes this is
    a. consensual validation.
    b. matching.
    c. complementarity.
    d. reciprocal positive evaluations.

MULTIPLE–CHOICE ANSWERS

1. c [259-260]	6. c [268-269]	11. d [280-281]	16. a [292]
2. c [259]	7. a [272]	12. c [284-285]	17. d [293-294]
3. d [262]	8. d [274-275]	13. d [288-289]	18. d [294-295]
4. d [260-262]	9. d [277]	14. d [290]	
5. a [265-266]	10. b [279]	15. a [291]	

IF YOU'D LIKE TO KNOW MORE: FURTHER SOURCES OF INFORMATION

Peele, Stanton and Brodsky, Archie, (1974, August). Interpersonal Heroin: Love Can Be an Addiction. PSYCHOLOGY TODAY, 22-26. The authors argue that middle–class dependency on spouses and lovers is akin to dependency on drugs. Discusses addictive vs. mature love.

Berscheid, Ellen and Walster, Elaine, (1972, March). Beauty and the Best. PSYCHOLOGY TODAY. 42-46. The way in which a variety of interpersonal behaviors are affected by the physical attractiveness of the participants is discussed.

Walster, Elaine, Piliavin, Jane, and Walster, G. Wm. (1973, September). The Hard-to-Get-Woman. PSYCHOLOGY TODAY, 80-83. Develops the hypothesis that men like women who are hard for other men to get, but easy for them. Explanations for the phenomenon are presented.

Solomon, R. C. (1981, October). The Love Lost in Cliches. PSYCHOLOGY TODAY, 83–94. Love is described as a relationship, as communication, as a contract, as a game, even as an illness. Whatever figure of speech lovers choose, they tend to express their love accordingly.

Go to http://topchoice.com/~psyche/lovetest/index.html   Do you want to know how you score on the Love Test? This site presents a questionnaire that is based on current research on love. After you complete the 68-item Love Test, you will be provided with your scores and information to help you interpret your scores.

Go to http://www.psychtests.com/soc_anx2.html   This site gives you a chance to measure your social anxiety. Social anxiety is closely related to need for affiliation, but it's obviously not the same thing. In what ways are these two concepts different?

THINKING CRITICALLY ABOUT INTERPERSONAL ATTRACTION

1. Look at a map of your campus and write down the names of several campus buildings. Try to list some buildings you visit frequently and some buildings you rarely or never visit. Now that you have a list of buildings, rate them for the degree to which you are familiar with each one. Secondly, rate each building for the degree to which you have a positive attitude toward it. If you compare your ratings of familiarity and your ratings of liking, you will probably find evidence for a mere exposure effect. Do you tend to like those buildings you're most familiar with? If you want to test the familiarity/liking relationship a little more formally, perhaps your instructor can help you gather more formal data and then help the class to calculate a correlation coefficient.

2. If you live in a residence hall, think about the friendship patterns that exist there. If you want to be a little more formal, you might draw a map of the rooms on your floor and summarize on the map who is friends with whom. Is there evidence to support the hypothesis that proximity leads to liking?

3. Think of your best friends and try to analyze what caused you to become friends. Can you think of instances where proximity, conditioned emotional responses, similarity, physical attractiveness, reciprocity, etc. influenced your attraction? Are the same factors important in your initial attraction to your friends compared to later phases of your relationship?

4. The romantic ideal, the notion that people base marriage decisions on "being in love," is perhaps more firmly established in the United States than elsewhere. Parents still have a great deal to say about the choice of a marriage partner in many countries, and in some cultures parents "arrange" marriages. An interesting question is the degree to which parents and their children agree as to the appropriateness of a particular potential mate. Who is in a better position to make a rational choice of a marriage partner—parents or their offspring? What would be a basis for parents' objecting seriously to the marriage (or dating) choices of their children?

5. Think of a question you got right on a multiple-choice exam. How many people in the class as a whole do you suppose got the question right? Next, think of a question you got wrong. Now how many people do you suppose got the question right? The hypothesis is that you will overestimate

the number of people who correctly answered the question you got right, and underestimate the number of people who correctly answered the one you got wrong. If you got it right, you wonder how anyone wouldn't get the answer. If you got it wrong, you wonder how anyone would know that! In each instance, you begin with the assumption that others know and believe the same things you know and believe, which is the definition of the false consensus effect. (See page 291 in your text.)

8

CLOSE RELATIONSHIPS:
FAMILY, FRIENDS, LOVERS, AND SPOUSES

CHAPTER OUTLINE: GETTING THE OVERALL PICTURE

Before reading the chapter, it may be helpful to examine the chapter outline. This will give you an idea of what is covered in the chapter and should help you organize your learning and review the material. You can also record notes on text sections under the outline headings for those sections.

I.   Initial Interdependent Relationships with Family and Friend—or Loneliness

    A. The First Relationships are a Family Matter

        1. Attachment Style: Learning self-esteem and trust

        2. The importance of other interactions between parents and their offspring

        3. Relationships between and among Siblings

    B. Social Diversity: A Critical Analysis—Felt Obligation toward Parents: Differences Within Families and Across Cultures

    C. Relationships Beyond the Family: Finding a Close Friend

        1. Childhood Friendships

        2. The development of close friendships in adolescence and adulthood

    D. Effects of Attachment Style on Adult Relationships

        1. Two working models and four attachment styles

        2. Attachment and behavior in adulthood

    E. Loneliness: Failing to Establish Close Relationships

        1. What are the consequences of loneliness?

111

2. How does loneliness development?

II. Romantic Relationships, Love, and Physical Intimacy

A. Romantic Relationships

1. Similarities between close friendships and romantic relationships

B. Beyond the Headlines: As Social Psychologists See It—Romance in the Workplace

C. What is this thing called Love?

1. Passionate love is very different from a close friendship

2. Falling in Love

3. Why love?

4. The many forms of love

D. Sexuality in Romantic Relationships

1. Changes in sexual attitudes and behavior

2. Is the sexual revolution over?

3. What is the effect of premarital sexual experience on later marriages?

III. Marriage: Moving Beyond Romance

A. Similarity and Marriage

B. Cornerstones of Social Psychology—Terman's Study of Husband-Wife Similarity and Marital Success

C. Marital Sex, Love, Parenthood, and Other Influences on General Satisfaction

1. Marital sex, love, and parenthood

2. Married versus single

3. Two career families

D. Troubled Relationships and the Effects of Marital Failure

1. What goes wrong?

2. Problems and solutions

3. Relationship failure: When dissatisfaction leads to dissolution

LEARNING OBJECTIVES: WHAT YOU SHOULD LEARN

As you are reading the chapter, these objectives provide page–by–page questions for you to answer. Answering the objectives should assure that you understand the essential material in the chapter.

1. Indicate the proportions of people who list "my one best person" as friend, family, or romantic partner. Discuss Bowlby's three attachment styles and relate them to interpersonal trust. List and describe the major traits of the secure, ambivalent, and avoidant attachment types. [305-308]

2. Discuss the implications for adolescence of Flannery and colleagues (1993) study of boys and girls in the fifth and ninth grades. How does liking of parents and virtuousness of teens relate to their love of their parents? Indicate the kind of parental behavior that teens respond to best. [308-309]

3. Relate individualism and collectivism to how teens respond to their parents in Anglo- and Mexican American families (Freeberg and Stein, 1996). Discuss how "Mom always liked you best." sums up sibling perceptions of one another's status with parents [309-311]

4. Describe how Manke and Plomin (1997) partialed the cognitive and personality similarities among siblings into genetic and shared environmental portions. Do siblings get more or less similar with age? Indicate the kind of siblings who have good and bad relations with family throughout their lives and the course of sibling relationships over the life span. [311-312]

5. Why do friends lie to each other? Describes the roles of proximity, similarity, and positive affect in friendships. Indicate the kind of attachment style that lends itself to the development of close friendships. Indicate which gender tends to have more close friendships. Describe the different topics that males and females talk about [312-315]

6. Give the percentages of people who display the different attachment styles. Discuss the importance of evaluation valence (positive or negative) of self and others in the formation of close relationships. Do secure people expect others will like them? Indicate the attachment style that is most androgynous. [316-317]

7. Contrast the secure, fearful avoidant, preoccupied, and dismissive attachment styles in terms of how they explain events in a relationship. Discuss Shaver's view of the relationship between infantile attachment styles and adult romantic attachment styles. Indicate the academic and social advantages of the secure. Can styles change? [317-319]

8. Define "loneliness", describe how it is measured, and indicate some traits of lonely people. Relate attachment styles to loneliness. [320-323]

9. Understand unrequited love and passionate romantic love. Explain the function of gazing.
    Compare the proportions of secure, ambivalent, and avoidant adult romantic lovers with the
    proportions of these styles in childhood. [324-331]

10. Historically, discuss how bonding relates to success at "passing on one's genes." Understand the
    three conditions of passionate love arousal and discuss the supposed role of skin color in mate
    selection and how life-time celibates and gay/lesbian people contradict evolutionary rules. [331]

11. State the role of mistaken emotions. Contrast companionate and passionate love. List and define
    the Hendricks' six love styles; provide example behaviors as well. Discuss how friendship relates
    to love. Understand relations among the corners of the love triangle. [331-3337]

12. Describe changes wrought by the sexual revolution. Describe the role of ethnicity and gender in
    partner selection and attitudes. [334-336]

13. Discuss the teen pregnancy legacy of the free love period. Describe the herpes and AIDS
    epidemics. Tract behavioral changes accompanying the spreads of HIV/AIDS. Discuss how
    premarital sex affects marriage and psychological health. [336-339]

14. Consider people's marriage aspirations as well as the evolving role of fathers and blended
    families. Discuss the role of similarity during the course of courtship and marriage. [339-341]

15. Describe the implications of settling for less than the perfect match. Discuss how similarity relates
    to happiness in marriage. Define the four states of early marriage uncovered by Johnson. [341-
    342]

16. Consider the effects of Johnson's four states of early marriage on marital satisfaction and
    parenthood. Look at intercourse frequency among partners whose relationships vary in length and
    commitment. Relate the decline in passionate love to relationship satisfaction and having children.
    [342-344]

17. Discuss how the marriage/happiness relationship has changed. Explain the current state of
    marriage, statistically speaking. Examine clashes of marital partners' personal interests, opinions,
    and coping strategies. [344-346]

18. Relate self-descriptions to marital satisfaction. Contrast the genders on sources of marital upset.
    List marital issues upon which conflicts can develop and changes in perceptions of partners'
    attributes. [346-350]

There's More Than First Meets Your Eyes: Understanding Figures in Your Text

*Turn to the figures in your text that are mentioned below and follow the discussion about how the
figures can increase you understanding of research and theory.*

1. Look at Figure 8.14 (p. 336) and the accompanying text. It displays a very strong gender difference and fits evolutionary theory very well. Notice that males' greater willing to engage in intercourse relative to females diminishes as the relationship lengthens. His way of passing his genes along is to have a lot of sex and invest as little of his resources in his offspring as is possible. Her way to pass along her genes is to get him committed so that his resources are available to her children. With the little commitment implied by a short-term relationship (leftmost bars), the difference is greatest, but as commitment increases as implied by lengthening relationship (rightmost bars), the difference diminishes.

2. Figure 18.17 (p. 345) and the accompanying text nicely outlines the costs and benefits of marriage. What it does not specify is the magnitude of the costs and benefits (which would be very hard to depict). Probably all marriages involve all the costs and benefits displayed, but the question is "how frequently and how intensely do the benefits outweigh the costs (or vice versa)?".

3. Figure 8.19 (p. 349) and the text that goes with it is interesting in that one course of action when a relationship is going bad is very definite (active) and the other (passive) is very ambiguous. Thus, the active mode either sets the relationship back on course or ends it, while the passive voice lengthens the limbo.

KEY TERMS: CONCEPTS YOU NEED TO UNDERSTAND

Write out the meaning of the following terms in your own words. Cover the right-hand portion of the exercise until you have finished, then check on the accuracy of your answers by comparing them with the definitions provided.

1.	Ludus	game playing [332]
2.	intimacy	the closeness that two people feel and the strength of the bond that holds them together [333]
3.	voice	the active approach to marital problems in which solutions are suggested [349]
4.	loneliness	an emotional and cognitive reaction to having fewer and less satisfying relationships than one desires [320s]
5.	dismissive attachment style	is characterized by a positive image of self (sometimes unrealistically positive) as being worthwhile and independent. [318]
6.	the sexual revolution	a period of sexual freedom during the second half of this century, peaking in the 1960s and extending into the 1970s [334]
7.	social phobia	a debilitating anxiety disorder in which interpersonal situations become sufficiently frightening that they are avoided [322]

MATCHING

Match each concept on the left side of the next page with an identifying phrase, word or sentence on the right side of the page. The answers may be found after the WHAT'S WRONG HERE? section.

A.	% of marrieds having sex twice/week	__	1.	50
B.	passive responses to disharmony	__	2.	painful blisters
C.	% of marriages that are remarriages	__	3.	Sociosexual Orientation Inventory
D.	passionate love	__	4.	friends vs. dating couples
E.	measure of sexual restrictiveness	__	5.	41
F.	herpes	__	6.	marrieds' similarities
G.	self-validation vs. positive feedback	__	7.	loyalty & neglect
H.	relatively unchanging over time	__	8.	Eros

WHAT'S WRONG HERE?

For each statement below indicate what needs to be changed in order to make the statement correct. You will find the answers at the end of the exercise, along with pages in the text where you can find more information.

1. Terman's famous study of married couples exposed the myth that married couples tend to be similar.

2. People who are passionately in love tend to regard their partners as close friends in whom they confide, but about whom they are respectful, not in awe.

3. Insecure-ambivalent style types tend to be emotionally consistent.

4. College students list a family member as the one closest person in their lives.

5. The socially skilled tend to be shy, modest, and self-conscious, which makes them non-threatening and, thus, socially successful.

6. Secure style types tend to be lonely because they are so competent they have a aura of not needing others.

7. "Securely attached," "avoidant," and "anxious ambivalent" are three of Bartholomew's styles.

8. "Cognitive therapy" and "social skills therapy" are useful for the elimination of the exploitive orientation to love.

9. Proximity is the rule of friendships and similarity is the rule of romantic relationships.

10. Friends tend to lie to each others to hide disloyalty.

11. Insecure ambivalent style types tend to have more positive friendship interactions because they are overly willing to let the friend have his/her way.

12. Relations between siblings tend to be close and stay close: none of this "Mom always liked you best." stuff.

13. When puberty arrives, parent/child relations become more understanding and pleasant, owing to the fact that parents are adults, and children are becoming adult.

14. Fortunately, the greater longevity of the U.S. white population has brought with it more willingness to care for aging parents.

15. Research shows that at children mature into the teens years, they express less negative affect, but, ironically, love their parents the less they like them.

16. Attachment in infancy and adjustment in high school is positive and high, supporting the notion that attachment style is constant throughout the life span.

MATCHING ANSWERS

5-A [341]; 7-B [349]; 1-C [350]; 8-D [330-331]; 3-E [335]; 2-F [338]; 4-G [327]; 6-H [339]

WHAT'S WRONG HERE? ANSWERS

1. Actually, he was among the first to point out the tendency for married couples to be similar. [340]
2. The description fits companionate love more, not passionate love. In passionate love, the partner is idolized and physiological arousal is a major component. It is thoughtless. [330]
3. That is exactly what they are not. [321-323]
4. No, its their romantic partner. [305]
5. This is actually the pattern of the unskilled. [320-322]
6. No, its the dismissing and fearful-avoidant who tend to be lonely. [306]
7. No, they are the attachment styles of Bowlby researched by Shaver and Hazan. [306]
8. Actually they are useful for the elimination of loneliness. [322]
9. No, though these two kinds of relationships are different, they do share similarity and proximity as important factors. [313 & 695]
10. No, they lie to make each other feel better. [312]
11. Actually it is the secure types who have positive interactions. [313]
12. Sibs can have rather rocky relations and may accuse Mom of favoritism toward other sibs. [310-311]
13. Unfortunately, as many people know, the opposite is most frequently true. [308]
14. It is and continues to be the more collectivistic cultures (Chinese and Mexican) that promote care for aging parents. [309-310]
15. Actually, negative affect increases (Flannery et al, 1993) and they love their parents to the extent that they like them (Galambos, 1992). [308]

16. In fact, the correlation is near zero and, though styles do stick around, they are not etched in stone. [319]

TRUE-FALSE

Indicate whether each of the following statements is true or false. If false, indicate why. Correct answers are found at the end of the exercise.

1. Men's marital satisfaction increases with more children, but women's decreases.

2. Only 6% of survey respondents say they have experienced unrequited love.

3. The genders are similar with regard to marital conflict. Both want to talk about it.

4. Over time single men have become less happy and married women more happy.

5. As one would expect, Dear Abby's "10 steps to a happy marriage" are just folk lore, unsupported by the research literature.

6. Men and women with high self-esteem respond to relationship failure by exiting.

7. Men's satisfaction with marriage depends on whether passion remains in the relationship.

8. One legacy of the sexual revolution is increased herpes and AIDS.

9. The advent of computer sexual surveys has increased false reporting.

10. Men and women tend to talk about the same things with friends: the opposite sex.

11. About 59% of people have secure attachment styles, while about 25% are insecure-avoidant, and only about 11% insecure-ambivalent.

12. Bartholomew added dismissive and preoccupied styles to the earlier classification by Shaver.

13. About 25% of employees report engaging in or being the target of sexual behavior in the workplace.

14. People describe close and casual friends in remarkably similar fashion.

TRUE-FALSE ANSWERS

1. True. [342]
2. False; it's 60%. [330]
3. False; men tend to want to avoid the issue. [344-345]

4. Not exactly; unmarried men are more happy than they used to be and married women are less happy. [342]
5. False; these steps are consistent with research results. [341]
6. True. [349]
7. False; men's satisfaction with marriage is unrelated to whether passion remains. [342]
8. True. [337-338]
9. False; computers increase anonymity and thus truthful reporting. [338-2]
10. False; the opposite sex is about the only thing their conversations have in common. [315]
11. True. [316]
12. True. [318]
13. False, it ranged from 40% (hiring decisions) to 68% (having sex with a co-worker). [326]
14. False; casual friends are valued as "fun" but close friends are valued for their generosity, sensitivity and honesty. [312]

FILL IN THE BLANKS: A GUIDED REVIEW

Mentally fill in each of the blanks in the following section while covering the answers in the margin. Check each answer against the answer in the margin by uncovering as you go along.

1. Secure attachment people tend to be _____.
    androgynous [316]
2. Shaver and Hazan hypothesized that when an adult enters a close relationship, his/her infantile _____ ___ will determine the nature of the adult relationship.
    attachment style [318]
3. Loneliness is associated with a lack of _____ in others.
    trust [320]
4. Gay men prefer partners who are _____ and lesbian women prefer partners who are _____.
    masculine, feminine [325]
5. _____ talk among romantic partners is most often found among secure partners.
    Baby [329]
6. People who report falling in love, indicate that the experience was beyond "my ____."
    control [330]
7. Women who were young adults during the sexual revolution report that they felt _____ to have sex.
    pressure [336]
8. Nowadays people are waiting until they are ___ before marrying.
    older [342]
9. Discovering differences after marriage tends to be a _____ process.
    slow [347]
10. Whether a woman changes her _____ is unrelated to the success of her marriage.
    name [343-344]
11. _____ of women are subjected to dating violence.
    40% [328]
12. A person with a positive self-image expects that others will _____ him or her.
    like [316]

MULTIPLE-CHOICE QUESTIONS: A PERSONAL QUIZ

After you have finished reading the chapter and done the other exercises in the STUDY GUIDE, take the quiz found below to test your knowledge. Indicate your answers by circling the letter of the chosen alternative. Check your answers against the answers provided at the end of the exercise.

1. Unlike secure and avoidant infants, ambivalent infants show ____ when the mother leaves and _____ when she returns.
   a. crying; laughing
   b. sulking; sulking
   c. crying; sulking
   d. crying; crying

2. Women tend to have ____ close friendships compared to men.
   a. fewer
   b. intense
   c. ambivalent
   d. more

3. Preoccupied people interpret relationship events in a negative way and report distress. Fearful avoidant people interpret events
   a. in the same way.
   b. in an entirely different way
   c. in the same way except that they are not distressed.
   d. in the same way except they are less negative.

4. According to Schachter's two factor theory,
   a. sex and compassion add up to love
   b. one may mistake another emotion for love
   c. love is in the eye of the beholder
   d. companionship and friendship constitute love

5. Loneliness is
   a. feeling alone.
   b. any feeling of solitary that is in fact valid.
   c. the unmet desire to engage in high quality/quantity close interpersonal relationships.
   d. the desire to have people around oneself regardless of circumstances.

6. The sexual revolution involved all of the following except one. Which is the EXCEPTION?
   a. fear of sexual disease
   b. acceptance of premarital sexual intercourse
   c. a greater tolerance of sexual practices in general
   d. a disappearance of sex differences in sexual experience

7. Cohabiting of unmarried couples is
   a. is a strong predictor of marital discord
   b. is on the decline
   c. is against the law in most states
   d. unrelated to marriage factors

8. What percent of women experience violence perpetrated by their dates?
   a. 40
   b. 10
   c. 75
   d. 90

9. If prospective lovers are aroused, they may
   a. immediately have intercourse.
   b. mistake the arousal for attraction to one another.
   c. become fearful of being around one another.
   d. paradoxically decide they are not for one another.

10. During the sexual revolution, women involved in it
    a. were as comfortable with free sex as men
    b. used sex to advance their own agendas
    c. often felt coerced by partners and social pressure
    d. were actually less willing to engage in sex than is now the case

11. Who shares household chores more equally?
    a. white middle class Americans
    b. lesbian couples
    c. Latino couples
    d. cohabiting couples

12. Which of the following is one of the Kendricks' six love styles?
    a. Agog
    b. Thanatos
    c. Pragma
    d. Alpha

13. A relatively common source of trouble in long term marriages is
    a. changing in different directions
    b. growing radically dissimilar
    c. having too much in common
    d. experiencing too much passion for each other

14. One index of whether a marriage is going well or badly is
    a. whether there is contact with in-laws
    b. whether there are children
    c. whether partners call each other by good or bad names
    d. whether a couple takes annual vacations

15. Passionate romantic love is characterized by
    a. falling head over heels.
    b. thoughtfulness.
    c. initially, little sexual chemistry.
    d. a certain comfortable feeling.

16. Manke and Plomin (1997) concluded what about sibling similarity?
    a. sibs are similar partly due to genetic similarity
    b. sibs are similar partly due to having similar friends
    c. sibs are dissimilar because they strive to be different
    d. sibs are dissimilar because they favor different parents

17. Age at first marriage has
    a. remained constant for generations
    b. varied from generation to generation
    c. was about 30 years in the 19th century but about 20 years in the 20th century
    d. has increased

18. What percent of married people say they never disagree?
    a. 40%
    b. 30%
    c. 12%
    d. 1.2%

19. Married people
    a. are universally unhappy.
    b. were happy, but no more.
    c. have changed from unhappy to happy in recent years.
    d. tend to be happier than unmarrieds.

20. Which of the following is the strongest reason for sexual incaution in the U.S.?
    a. alcohol
    b. culture
    c. lack of contraceptive availability
    d. sexual ignorance

MULTIPLE CHOICE ANSWERS

1. d [307]	6. a [335-336]	11. b [342]	16. a [310-311]
2. d [313-314]	7. d [339]	12. c [332-333]	17. d [342-343]
3. c [318-319]	8. a [328]	13. a [347]	18. d [344]
4. b [331]	9. b [331]	14. c [347-348]	19. d [342]
5. c [320]	10. c [336-337]	15. a [330]	20. a [337-338]

IF YOU'D LIKE TO KNOW MORE: FURTHER SOURCES OF INFORMATION

Goleman, D. (1996, Jan.). What's Your Emotional I.Q. READERS DIGEST, 49-52. Most of the problems that people have in close relationships would be solved by developing a high emotional I.Q. When you read this short article it will be apparent that at least some of the components of high emotional I.Q. can be learned.

Edwards, R. (1995, Feb). New Tools Help Gauge Marital Success. MONITOR OF THE AMERICAN PSYCHOLOGICAL ASSOCIATION, 6. Dealing well with conflict is the key to marital success. This article indicates that two-thirds of marriages survive affairs, but there is a gender difference. Women who have affairs are more likely to be emotionally involved, thus making them more detached from their spouses. Men have less patience with the aftermath of an affair.

Tavris, C. (1988, Nov.). Coping with Jealousy. PSYCHOLOGY TODAY, 302. Carol Tavris is well-known for her theorizing about anger. More recently she has turned her attention to jealousy. Here she provides useful information about coping with jealousy.

Roberts, M. (1988, March). Be All That You Can Be. PSYCHOLOGY TODAY, 28-29. As the text indicates, one of the major problems facing lonely people is lack of the kinds of skills that allow success in general and social success in particular. This article indicates which, among the several self-improvement methods available, really does work.

Ansen. D. (April 27, 1998). Not a classic date Movie: James Toback's scorching comedy of relationships. NEWSWEEK. So you wonder what would happen if a guy was switching between two girl friends. Wonder no more. Read this article or see the movie, Two Girls and a Guy. It's evolutionary theory on the big screen.

Bower, B. (1997). Social sense may heed uneven inheritance. SCIENCE NEWS, vol. 151, June 14, p. 365. Based on research on Turner's Syndrome (all or part of one X chromosome is missing) researchers surmise that there may be a place on the X chromosome that houses a gene for social skills. Turner's Syndrome females with a damaged X chromosome inherited from their mothers seem to lack social skills.

Hoekstra, D. & Gillis, M. (1999) Some couples are merry not be married. Associated Press (PEORIA JOURNAL STAR, January 3, p. B7). So what what good is cohabiting? It doesn't make better marriages and it doesn't tend to last long. This article has little good to say about it.

Go to http://www.online-romance.com/ Cupid has invaded the Web. Visit this site for romantic postcards, a Lovers Questionnaire, and much more.

Go to http://www.arach.net.au/users/morria/reject.htm Forget David Letterman. Here is what women and men really mean by the rejection lines they use.

Go to http://home.netinc.ca/~sexorg/ "This Web Site is dedicated to the advancement of knowledge of human sexuality, in all of its diversity" (first page). Indeed it is. There are research questionnaires, ask a Doc about your problem, a Facts of Life Netline, and Sexology Links.

Go to http://www.as.org/as/ A dating service online. Yes, you can build a profile in the hope of finding Mr. or Miss right. Includes services for heterosexual and gay/lesbian people.

Go to http://www.indiana.edu/~kinsey/ This site is an inroad into Indiana University's famous Kinsey Institute. You can find out about their library, publications/research, clinics and exhibitions.

THINKING CRITICALLY ABOUT CLOSE RELATIONS

1. Famed psychologist Albert Bandura talks of how chance can shape our lives. In his own case, had he not been playing golf on a particular golf course, on a particular day, at a particular time, he wouldn't have met the women he married. Think about who you are likely to marry (or, if you are married, who you happened to marry). Will it (or did it) have anything to do with your decision to attend the university where you now matriculate, the job you happened to have, the party you happened to attend? Think about how you would have married someone else had circumstances been different (and go tell your spouse how fortunate you've been!) or think about how different the person you might have married would have been compared to whom you will likely marry. Now write your thoughts down.

2. Which pattern do you fit best: secure, avoidant, preoccupied, or dismissing? It's forced choice; choose one. Now indicate your behaviors and emotions that make you fit the pattern, and what it is about your up-bringing that determined your pattern.

3. Similarity is best in interpersonal relationships. That is a constant (and legitimate) theme of your text. However, when does this general rule not hold? When might people have a better, more lasting relationship because they possess different, but complementary, characteristics (one is talkative, the other is taciturn). You might want to think in terms of friends you know or dating/married couples you know.

4. How important is sex to a marriage? Robert Sternberg implies that of the three most important factors in a successful marriage—intimacy (communication), commitment to the relationship, and passion (sex)—passion is the only one that can be missing. Take a side. Argue that "good sex" is essential to a successful marriage; sex, good or bad, is the only ingredient that can be left out of a successful marriage; or (here's a tough one) sex is more essential than either intimacy or commitment.

5. Are we crazy to marry for love? In other cultures, marriages are arranged, the families of the betrothed become as one, divorce is nearly taboo, and couples come to love each other during the course of marriage. Who has it right, us (U.S. mainstream culture) or them? Defend your position.

SOCIAL INFLUENCE: HOW WE CHANGE OTHERS' BEHAVIOR--AND HOW THEY CHANGE OURS

CHAPTER OUTLINE: GETTING THE OVERALL PICTURE

Before reading the chapter, it may be helpful to examine the chapter outline. This will give you an idea of what is covered in the chapter and should help you organize your learning and review the material. You can also record notes on text sections under the outline headings for those sections.

I. Conformity: Group Influence in Action

    A. Cornerstones of Social Psychology—Asch's Research on Conformity: Social Pressure—The Irresistible Force?

    B. Factors Affecting Conformity: Variables That Determine the Extent to Which We "Go Along"

        1. Cohesion and Conformity: Accepting Influence From Those We Like

        2. Conformity and Group Size. Why More Is Better with Respect to Social Influence

        3. Type of social norm in operation: What we should do versus what we actually do

    C. The Bases of Conformity: Why We Often Choose to "Go Along

        1. The Desire to Be Liked: Normative Social Influence

        2. The Desire to Be Right: Informational Social Influence

        3. Justifying Conformity: The Cognitive Consequences of Going Along with the Group

    D. The Need for Individuality and the Need for Control: Why, Sometimes, We Choose *Not* to Go Along

    E. Beyond the Headlines: As Social Psychologists See It—Dress Codes Versus Personal Freedom: When Norms Collide

    F. Minority Influence: Does the Majority Always Rule?

III. Compliance: To Ask—Sometimes—Is to Receive

    A. Compliance: The Underlying Principles

    B. Tactics Based on Friendship or Liking: Ingratiation

    C. Tactics Based on Commitment or Consistency: The Foot in the Door and The Low Ball

    D. Tactics Based on Reciprocity: The Door in the Face and the "That's-Not-All" Approach.

    E. Tactics Based on Scarcity: Playing Hard to Get and the Fast-Approaching Deadline Technique

    F. Other Tactics for Gaining Compliance: Complaining and Putting Others in a Good Mood

    G. Individual Differences in the Use of Social Influence: Do Different Persons Prefer Different Tactics?

IV. Obedience: Social Influence by Demand

    A. Destructive Obedience: Some Basic Findings

    B. Destructive Obedience: Its Social Psychological Basis

    C. Destructive Obedience: Resisting Its Effects

LEARNING OBJECTIVES: WHAT YOU SHOULD LEARN

As you are reading the chapter, these objectives provide page–by–page questions for you to answer. Answering the objectives should assure that you understand the essential material in the chapter.

1. Define conformity. Describe explicit and implicit norms. Indicate why we need to conform. Outline the Asch procedure for studying conformity. Know the results of Asch's studies (percentages conforming). [356-359]

2. Provide some explanations for failure to conform. Describe the "ally" effect. Contrast public conformity to private acceptance. Define cohesiveness and indicate how it affects conformity. Discuss the "group size" controversy. [350-351]

3. Define "descriptive" and "injunctive norms" and when and why the latter are effective. Describe Cialdini's and colleagues' (Reno et al., 1993) "drop the fast food bag" study in which injunctive and descriptive norms were compared. [361-362]

4. Describe the Southern/Western "code of honor" and its origins. Discuss the Cohen's and Nisbett's (1997) "murder or thief" letter of application study and its implications for the code, as well as its power and persistence as a norm. [362-364]

5. List some reasons for conformity. Contrast normative and informational social influence. Describe the procedure and results of the Robert S. Baron and colleagues (1996) study involving the facial drawings shown for short and long periods. [364-365]

6. How do we justify conforming and how do we deal with it after we conform? Indicate the role of culture in justification of conformity. [365-366]

7. Describe the role of "need for control" and "need to individuate" in resistance to conformity. Contrast collectivistic and individualistic cultures in amount of conformity. [366-367]

8. Describe the tension between the desire for control and to be unique on the one hand and the desire to be liked and to be accurate on the other. Discuss the "visit to the Vatican" where descriptive and injunctive norms clashed. [368-369]

9. Discuss the three avenues to minority influence on majorities. Do they rely on informational or normative influence or both? Define "systematic processing" and its role in minority influence. [369-370]

10. Describe the procedure and results of the Zdaniuk and Levine (1996) "comprehensive exam" study and its implications for minority status and systematic processing. Discuss the value for the majority of minority opposition. [370-372]

11. Define compliance. How frequently used a form of social influence is it? Identify the "compliance professionals" and describe their six basic principles. Impression management is often used for what purpose? [372-373]

12. Describe methods of flattery. Discuss the foot-in-the-door technique and the compliance principle it rests on. Discuss the "low ball" technique and the Cialdini and colleagues (1978) "early hour experiment" study. [373-374]

13. Describe the "door-in-the-face" technique and its reliance on reciprocity. Discuss Cialdini and colleagues (1975)" work with juvenile delinquents" study. Describe the "that's not all" technique and relate it to reciprocity. [374-376]

14. Discuss the rarity of commodities and the fast-approaching deadline techniques. Describe the William's and colleagues (1993) "hard to get", "easy to get" job-candidate study. How did the low-qualified, hard to get candidate fare? [376-377]

15. Why does the deadline technique work? Define "complaining" and indicate how it can be used as a social influence tactic. List and describe the Alicke et al's (1992) types of complaints and their frequency of use. [377-378]

16. Discuss why people complain and gender differences in response to complaints. Describe how manipulating others' mood gains compliance with reference to Rind's and Bordia's (1995) happy faces study. Was there a gender difference? [378-379]

17. Discuss the Affective Infusion Model. Indicate how Forgas' (1998) study supports this model (subjects found a mood altering sheet of paper). How did "depth of thinking" influence results? Define "pressure tactics." [379-381]

18. Relate individual differences in preferences for compliance techniques to the Big 5 of Caldwell and Burger (1997). Define "need for cognition" and relate it to success at influencing others. Define Obedience and the "velvet glove". Is obtaining obedience limited to the powerful? [381-382]

19. What inspired Milgram to do his famous obedience studies? Describe the procedure of his "pounding on the wall study." What % obeyed in this study? Compare obedience in the U. S. to that of other countries. Consider the ethical questions related to Milgram's research. [383-385]

20. Discuss the causes of destructive obedience, particularly the less obvious ones, gradualism and the pace of events. Know the role of perceived responsibility for the outcome of obeying. Consider disobedient models, challenging the expertise of authority, and knowledge of obedience research in resisting orders. [385-387]

There's More Than First Meets Your Eyes: Understanding Figures in Your Text

Turn to the figures in your text that are mentioned below and follow the discussion about how the figures can increase you understanding of research and theory.

1. Look at Figure 9.5 (p. 362) and the accompanying text. Except that activating a norm reduces littering (right most bars versus the rest), basically the whole story is in the center two bars. Activating a descriptive norm reduces litter only in a clean environment.

2. Look at Figure 9.6 (p. 364) and the text that goes with it. When honor is mentioned as the justification for murder, there is a big difference in the provision of job information between South/West and North. But when theft is mentioned, the provision of information is about the same for all regions.

3. Look at Figure 9.7 (p. 366) and the text referring to it. When it is not important to be accurate, conformity is uninfluenced by how certain participants were about their judgments. However, when it is important to be accurate, their conformity goes way up when they are uncertain. When their judgments are important, they want to avoid giving wrong answers.

4. Figure 9.8 (p. 368) straightforwardly shows an important cultural difference in conformity. Regardless of group size, in collectivistic cultures, where group affiliation is terribly important, conformity is greater.

5. Look at Figure 9.10 (p. 371) and the text that explains it. The fewer allies one has, the more social pressure one feels (left bars, "0"). As logic would have it, as the pressure due to being in a distinct minority goes up, the more it behooves one to think carefully about one's position (right bars, "0").

6. Figure 9.13 (p. 380) displays an ironic finding. People actually comply more when happy than when sad, if the requester is impolite. Is it that when we are feeling good we can be charitable to a poor, surly person?

KEY TERMS: CONCEPTS YOU NEED TO UNDERSTAND

Write out the meaning of the following terms in your own words. Cover the right-hand portion of the exercise until you have finished, then check on the accuracy of your answers by comparing them with the definitions provided.

1.	conformity	changing behavior to adhere to that of other persons in one's group [356-357]
2.	compliance	getting others to say "yes" to our requests [357 & 372]
3.	obedience	an authority figure simply orders people to do something and they do it [357 & 382]
4.	systematic processing	the deep cognitive processing that may accompany being in a minority [370]
5.	cohesiveness	the degree of attraction felt by individuals toward some group [360]
6.	"That's not all!"	the offer of a bonus added to some "deal" before the target can say whether she or he is interested in the "deal" [375]
7.	foot-in-the-door	induce a person to comply with a small request thereby increase the chances she or he will comply with a subsequent large request [374]
8.	individuation	desire to be distinguished in some respects from others [367]
9.	normative and informational social influence	altering behavior to fit expectations of others and being influenced by information received from others in order to be "right" [364-365]
10.	door-in-the-face	start with a large request and then switch to a small one [374]
11.	fast approaching deadline technique	stating a time limit within which a product can be purchased for a specific price [376]
12.	low-ball	a very good deal becomes less good after a customer commits to buy [374]
13.	ingratiation	getting others to like us so that they are more willing to grant our requests [373]

MATCHING

*Match each concept on the left side of the page with an identifying phrase, word or sentence on the right side of the page. The answers may be found after the **WHAT'S WRONG HERE?** section.*

A.	door-in-the-face	___ 1.	making demands, blowing up, etc.
B.	foot-in-the-door	___ 2.	small request then large one
C.	conformity research	___ 3.	models of disobedience
D.	pressure tactics	___ 4.	a large request then a small request
E.	Affect Infusion Model (AIM)	___ 5.	line judgments
F.	smiley face	___ 6.	motivation for and enjoyment of effortful cognitive activities
G.	need for cognition	___ 7.	obligations
H.	source of non-compliance to orders	___ 8.	larger tips
I.	one of six categories of complaints	___ 9.	priming of associations and memories related to current mood

WHAT'S WRONG HERE?

For each statement below indicate what needs to be changed in order to make the statement correct. You will find the answers at the end of the exercise, along with pages in the text where you can find more information.

1. Minorities may expect to exert some influence on the larger majority of a group if they are careful to vary their position.

2. Social norms always change from generation to generation.

3. Conformity tends to increase up to group size 8.

4. If minorities are to exert influence they must "stick to their guns" and not give an inch.

5. A study showed that job candidates with two job offers in hand did worse than those with no offers.

6. In the Asch lines studies, 24% of subjects went along with the false judgment at least once.

7. We tend not to obey conventions like "don't cut in line", "don't stand too close to strangers", and "don't arrive at parties too early".

8. The "velvet glove" technique involves especially harsh orders.

9. The Milgram obedience study covered in your text involved a learner with a heart condition who cried to be let out repeatedly.

10. In the famous Asch conformity experiments, participants judged the movement of a point of light presented in total darkness.

11. Need for control and for individuation work together with the need to be right and to be liked in promoting conformity.

12. Reciprocity is a way to resist others' influence.

13. Rational argument, ingratiation, inspirational appeals and reciprocity are among the pressure tactics investigated by Lennox and Wolfe (1984).

MATCHING ANSWERS

4-A [374]; 2-B [374]; 5-C [358]; 1-D [380]; 9-E [379]; 8-F [379]; 6-G [382]; 3-H [387]; 7-I [378]

WHAT'S WRONG HERE? ANSWERS

1. Minority influence depends in part on consistency. [370]
2. Actually, like the South/West norm of honor, they can be passed from generation to generation. [363]
3. No, it may increase well beyond that group size. [360-361]
4. To the contrary, they should not be rigid and dogmatic. [370]
5. Actually it was the other way around due to the "hard to get" phenomenon. [376]
6. It was 76%. [358]
7. We tend to comply with these conventions. [357]
8. Actually it is requests rather than orders. [382]
9. No, it was only pounding on the wall [384]
10. It was some lines of varying length. [358-359]
11. Need for control and for individuation is opposed by the need to be right and to be liked. [368]
12. No, it is tit for tat; you do something for me and I'll do something for you. [374]
13. Rational argument, ingratiation, inspirational appeals and reciprocity are among the influence tactics chosen by different people as investigated by Caldwell and Burger (1997). [381]

TRUE-FALSE

Indicate whether each of the following statements is true or false. If false, indicate why. Correct answers are found at the end of the exercise.

1. In the Reno et al. study, on the parking lot and off the lot, descriptive norm adherence led to helping.

2. The "ally" effect refers to cases where a person faced with a majority who make an absurd judgment have one other who disagrees with the majority.

3. Special uniforms, badges, titles and so forth do little to increase the power of authority.

4. Gradual escalation of shock levels in the Milgram experiment served to lower obedience.

5. Milgram used a kind of reaction time task in which the slower "player" was shocked.

6. The desire to be liked and the desire to be right are two powerful reasons why we conform.

7. At the Vatican, visitors are welcomed dressed in every way from very casual to formal.

8. Only 12% of participants in the Milgram experiment covered in your text obeyed fully.

9. When group size begins to get beyond three or four members, targets of influence attempts begin to suspect collusion among other members.

10. Among the experiments run by Milgram one was in a rundown office building.

11. Minorities are sources of both informational and normative influence on majorities.

TRUE-FALSE ANSWERS

1. False; it was adherence to the injunctive norm. [361]
2. True. [359]
3. False; these symbols of authority increase an authority figure's power. [385]
4. False; it served to increase obedience. [385]
5. False; he used a long panel of switches increasing, left to right, at 15 volt per switch; the participant delivered shock upon an incorrect response on the part of the learner. [384]
6. True. [364-365]
7. False; casual dress was forbidden. [368-369]
8. False; it was 65%. [384]
9. False; it is now known that conformity may increase even with large increase in group size. [361]
10. True. [384]
11. True. [370]

FILL IN THE BLANKS: A GUIDED REVIEW

Mentally fill in each of the blanks in the following section while covering the answers in the margin. Check each answer against the answer in the margin by uncovering as you go along.

1. Public _____ and private _____ do not always go together.

conformity; acceptance [359]

2. Cialdini and colleagues believe that in general _____ norms achieve more compliance than _____ norms.

injunctive; descriptive [361]

3. The "cover study" presented to subjects in Milgram's obedience experiments so that they would not be suspicious was that they would be participating in a _____ experiment.

learning [384]

4. The principle of _____ is partly behind the "that's not all" technique ("Here's an extra, now its your turn to give").

reciprocity [375-376]

5. Subjects on the Milgram experiments were more likely to disobey if they were made to feel _____ for any harm coming to the "learner" and if they had been present with a person who acted as a _____ of disobedience.

responsible; model [386-387]

6. Being distinguished from others is called _____.

individuation [367]

7. We may alter our _____ of a situation to _____ conforming in it.

perceptions; justify [365-366]

8. In _____ cultures people conform more than in _____ cultures.

collectivistic; individualistic [366]

MULTIPLE-CHOICE QUESTIONS: A PERSONAL QUIZ

After you have finished reading the chapter and done the other exercises in the STUDY GUIDE, take the quiz found below to test your knowledge. Indicate your answers by circling the letter of the chosen alternative. Check your answers against the answers provided at the end of the exercise.

1. Why is conformity sometimes not a good thing?
   a. It isn't; we should always do it.
   b. It may threaten individuation on our part.
   c. Deviating from the behavior of the majority is necessarily productive.
   d. It is best that people all behave differently.

2. "Private acceptance" refers to
   a. going along with others to save yourself embarrassment.
   b. going along within oneself, but openly defying the group.
   c. actually coming to think and feel as the group does.
   d. actually declaring publicly that you believe internally as the group does.

3. To show that "public conformity" and "private acceptance" were different, Asch (1957) had subjects
    a. announce their answers to a good friend.
    b. write their answers down, rather than speak them aloud.
    c. speak their answers aloud, rather than write them down.
    d. publish their answers in the student newspaper.

4. According to Alicke and colleagues (1992), people complain for all of the following reasons, except one. Which is NOT a reason for complaining?
    a. to get sympathy
    b. to show others up
    c. to get advice
    d. to get information

5. The study of obedience in other countries revealed
    a. that obedience is relatively high in the U.S.
    b. that obedience is relatively low in the U.S.
    c. that Americans are unique in the way they obey
    d. that the tendency to obey is quite general

6. According to the notion of "consistency"
    a. if a person complies with a small request, she has the right to refuse a subsequent large request.
    b. if a requester "backs down" from a large request to a small one, the target of the request may feel compelled to grant the second request.
    c. if the target of a request refuses an initial large request, he may feel that he will "look bad" if he refuses a subsequent small request.
    d. if a target of initial small request grants the same, she may feel obligated to grant a subsequent large request.

7. Which is an example of an unwritten norm?
    a. "Posted speed is 65 MPH—No tolerance!"
    b. "Residents above the age of 70 are granted a lower tax rate by order of the city council."
    c. "One should not break into a line of people waiting."
    d. "Students not registered by Sept. 15 will be charged a late fee."

8. Widespread disobeying of social norms would lead to
    a. social chaos.
    b. teaching children not be slavish conformists.
    c. lowering the authoritarianism of the population.
    d. more questioning of the government than other institutions.

9. Which of the following is true regarding the original experiments on obedience by Stanley Milgram?
   a. The experimenter pressured subjects to continue the experiment even when the "victim" signaled distress.
   b. The subjects were always told that since they were the ones pushing the switches, they (the subjects) were responsible for the victim's welfare.
   c. Strong shocks were actually delivered to the victim.
   d. When the experiment was moved from Yale to a rundown office building in a nearby city, the level of obedience was sharply reduced.

10. According to Alicke et al. (1992) what is the most frequent reason people give for complaining?
    a. seeking sympathy
    b. seeking information
    c. seeking advice
    d. expressing frustration

11. When Klotz and Alicke (1993) consulted same sex friends, opposite sex friends, and dating couples about their complaints, who was most supportive?
    a. neither gender more than the other
    b. males
    c. females.
    d. one gender or the other depending on circumstances.

12. Social influence is
    a. being influenced by others.
    b. the influence of society on us.
    c. influencing how society operates and determining how it will operate in the future.
    d. the efforts on the part of one person to alter the behavior or attitudes of one or more others.

13. Conformity occurs when
    a. individuals change their behavior in order to fit that of other persons in their group.
    b. individuals adhere to conventions of a society such as wearing clothes.
    c. individuals influence each other.
    d. individuals mimic each other.

14. A "social norm" is a
    a. written rule.
    b. law that has legal status in court.
    c. spoken and unspoken rules concerning how we ought to behave.
    d. the same as a taboo.

15. How are culture and cognitive justification for conformity related?
    a. they are not related; they are independent
    b. pressure for justification may be weaker in collectivistic cultures
    c. pressure for justification may be stronger in collectivistic cultures
    d. pressure for justification may be weaker in individualistic cultures

16. What percentage of Asch's control subjects made mistakes in judging the lines?
    a. 25%
    b. 5%
    c. 45%
    d. 0%

17. The "that's not all" technique
    a. is untested.
    b. really does work, according to research.
    c. has been shown to be ineffective by research.
    d. has generated mixed results in research.

18. What percent of Asch's participants voiced agreement with the collaborators false judgments?
    a. 37%
    b. 76%
    c. 5%
    d. 14%

19. Which of the following reduced obedience in the Milgram studies to 30%?
    a. learner complained of pain.
    b. conducting the experiment away from prestigious Yale University.
    c. pounding on a wall by the victim.
    d. having to actually place the victim's hand on a shock plate.

20. The power of authority in the Milgram's experiments was in large part due to
    a. his large stature
    b. his title of "professor"
    c. his release of participants from responsibility
    d. his insistence that he along was fully responsible

MULTIPLE CHOICE ANSWERS

1. b [367]	6. d [373]	11. c [378]	16. b [358]
2. c [359]	7. c [357]	12. d [356]	17. b [375]
3. b [359]	8. a [357]	13. a [357]	18. a [358]
4. b [378]	9. a [383-384]	14. c [357]	19. d [385]
5. d [385]	10. d [378]	15. b [365-366]	20. c [385-386]

IF YOU'D LIKE TO KNOW MORE: FURTHER SOURCES OF INFORMATION

Powell, B., Post, T. & Nordland, R. (1995, Nov.). Lessons of Nuremberg...The Trial of the Century...The Crimes of Bosnia. NEWSWEEK, 15. At Nuremberg, Nazi war criminals pleaded innocent by "virtue" of blind obedience. They claimed that "we were just following orders." Have humans learned from Nuremberg so that now they take responsibility for their actions rather than claim some authority figure was responsible? Unfortunately no. Witness the "ethnic cleansing" of Bosnia (and later Kosovo) which may not even come to trial.

Fram, A. (Associated Press, 1995, Dec. 23) "Good Meetings," But No Budget. PEORIA JOURNAL STAR, A2. What social influence methods have the Democrats and Republicans used on each other to end the budget freeze caused by disagreements over the deficit? Complain, complain, complain. As of Dec. 23, 1995, they had at least become more cordial. By the time you read this (and look up the article?), you will know how the stalemate was resolved. Did they resort to reciprocity?

Remley, A. (1988, Oct.). From Obedience to Independence: Parents Used to Raise Their Children to be Dutiful. PSYCHOLOGY TODAY, 54. The times have changed. Now parents are raising their children to be self-reliant, rather than obedient.

Pines, M. (1981, May). Unlearning Blind Obedience in German Schools. PSYCHOLOGY TODAY, 59-65. Have the German people learned from the lessons of World War II? Apparently they have.

Coleman, A. (1980, May). Flattery Won't Get You Everywhere. PSYCHOLOGY TODAY, 80-82. The author covers the limitations of flattery (ingratiation), including when it might backfire.

Herbert, W. (1985, March). Cyranoids: Artificial Selves. PSYCHOLOGY TODAY, 6-7. Remember the story of Cyrano de Bergerac, he of the preposterous proboscis? Just before he died, Stanley Milgram began to investigate a new way to influence people: have someone else speak your words for you, then you can't be held responsible.

Krauthammer, C. Why we admire Tiger Woods. READERS DIGEST, July, 1997, 71-75. Models are such potent sources of social influence and none are seen as more important examples for young people than famous athletes. According to this author, Woods is such a welcomed model, because, among other things, he models respect and love for parents. And, like Michael Jordan, he is a person of color with whom white kids can and do identify. There can be no more powerful way to break down racial-barriers than cross-race identification.

Go to http://www.salesdoctors.com/ Home page of a sales magazine written by sales experts to help people sell more. So its about compliance techniques from the lips of the supersellers.

Go to http://www.uiowa.edu/~commstud/resources/advertising.html This site is your avenue into the world of advertising. Included are gender and race as factors in sales.

Go to http://www.antitelemarketer.com/ Everything you ever wanted to know about getting rid of telemarketers. It is sort of the flip side of sales techniques. It includes "tormenting techniques" and dealing with hang up calls.

THINKING CRITICALLY ABOUT SOCIAL INFLUENCE

1. People may wonder, is it "bad" to conform? If so, there are a lot of "bad" people out there, because almost everyone shows some conformity. Indicate why it is that all of us who wish to survive and prosper must display some minimal level of conformity. What about those of who are "rebels," never yield to conformity pressure? Tell why such behavior is not reasonable.

2. Is the tendency to obey the commands of authority figures a cultural thing, occurring mostly in highly authoritarian societies, such as Germany is alleged to represent? Maybe it is more universal, true of humans regardless of culture. Decide which of these alternatives is more true and defend your decision.

3. Imposing a deadline is not good strategy for influencing some people. Procrastinators may constitute such people. As deadlines approach, they seem impervious to pleas from friends and colleagues that they get their part done. What motivates such seemingly self-destructive behavior? Indicate why you think that procrastinators put things off until the last moment....and be careful to be critical about the claim "I work best under the gun." (What's wrong with this claim?)

4. Ingratiation is an interesting social influence tool. Sometimes it works and sometimes it might backfire. Outline the circumstances in which it will tend to get the ingratiator what she/he wants, and the conditions in which it might backfire and lower the probability of getting what is wanted. Even when it works, are its benefits ever as great as being genuine with others?

5. Can you come up with some additional anti-compliance techniques not implied by your text? It literally pays to be able to resist. For example, telemarketers are fast talkers. When they call one of us (Allen) he says very rapidly "I'm sorry, we take no solicitations over the phone." and hangs up. Once when one of us was soliciting donations for a charity (Allen), he approached a potential donor and was confronted with "Hi! What can I do you out of?" Think about switching reciprocity, reversing commitment, and assuming expertise about the sales item.

10

PROSOCIAL BEHAVIOR: PROVIDING HELP TO OTHERS

CHAPTER OUTLINE: GETTING THE OVERALL PICTURE

Before reading the chapter, it may be helpful to examine the chapter outline. This will give you an idea of what is covered in the chapter and should help you organize your learning and review the material. You can also record notes on text sections under the outline headings for those sections.

I. Responding to an Emergency: Why Are Bystanders Sometimes Helpful, Sometimes Indifferent?

    A. Cornerstones of Social Psychology—Darley and Latané: Why Bystanders Don't Respond

    B. Providing Help—Yes or No? Five Essential Steps in the Decision Process

        1. Step One—Noticing the emergency

        2. Step Two—Interpreting an emergency as an emergency

        3. Step Three—Assume that helpfulness is your responsibility

        4. Step Four—Knowing what to do

        5. Step Five—Deciding to help

    C. Social Diversity: A Critical Analysis—Big Cities versus Small Towns: Does Prosocial Behavior Depend in Part on Where You Live?

    D. Situational Factors that Enhance or Inhibit Helping: Attraction, Attributions, and Prosocial Models

        1. Helping those you like

        2. Attributions of victim responsibility

        3. Models of prosocial behavior: The power of positive examples

II. The Helpers and Those Who Receive Help

    A. Helping as a Function of the Bystander's Emotional State

        1. Positive emotions and their effect on prosocial behavior

        2. Negative emotions and their effect on prosocial behavior

    B. Dispositional Differences in Prosocial Responding

        1. Empathy: A basic requirement

        2. How does empathy develop and why do people differ in empathy?

        3. Beyond empathy: Additional personality components of empathy

    C. Beyond the Headlines: As Social Psychololgists See It—Ordinary People Sometimes do Extraordinary Things

    D. Volunteering: Motivations for Long Term Help

        1. Volunteering on the basis of a variety of motives

        2. Volunteering as a matter of having an altruistic personality

    E. Who Receives Help and How Do They React to Being Helped?

        1. Gender as a factor in who receives help

        2. Asking for Help

        3. How does it feel to receive help?

III. Explaining Prosocial Behavior: Why Do People Help?

    A. Empathy-Altruism: It Feels Good to Help Those in Need

    B. Negative-State Relief: It Reduces One's Negative Affect to Relieve a Stressful Situation

    C. Empathic Joy: Successful Helping as a Way to Arouse Positive Affect

    D. Genetic Determinism: Helping Maximizes the Survival of Genes Like One's Own

LEARNING OBJECTIVES: WHAT YOU SHOULD LEARN

As you are reading the chapter, these objectives provide page–by–page questions for you to answer. Answering the objectives should assure that you understand the essential material in the chapter.

1. Describe some real life instances of helping in an emergency and failure to help. Discuss the Kitty Genovese case and Darley and Latane's "diffusion of responsibility" explanation of it. Describe bystander apathy. [394-398]

2. Know the general procedure and results of Darley's and Latane's "seizure study." Discuss how it illustrates the "bystander effect" and supports "diffusion of responsibility". [398]

3. Compare a face-to-face encounter with an actual emergency to an armchair encounter (via reading) in terms of deciding what to do. Discuss "noticing" the first step toward helping, by reference to the Good Samaritan study. [399-401]

4. Consider step 2, interpreting a situation as an emergency, with reference to the ambiguity of the Kitty Genovese case. Indicate how embarrassment might play a role in failure to interpret a situation as an emergency. Describe the smoke study procedure and explain how "pluralistic ignorance" explains its results. [401-403]

5. Indicate whose presence limits social inhibitions against interpreting a situation as an emergency. Know whether prosocial behavior depends on being in an urban or rural area. Define "stimulus over-load." Discuss Levine's (1994) study of the effects on prosocial behavior of population density. [403-404]

6. Outline the factors involved in assuming responsibility for helping (step 3) and knowing what to do (step 4). Who is likely to assume responsibility and know what to do? Name some emergencies where intervention to help can be dangerous. What kind of people is an individual likely to help? Describe step 5. [404-405]

7. Indicate how much help a person received if the help request (last dime method) implied that he was gay versus "straight" (Shaw and colleagues, 1994). Compare the help rates expected when a victim of an emergency is blamed for it, relative to blame attributed to an non-victim source. [406-407]

8. Describe what religious fundamentalists recommended to gay men and unwed mothers regarding an unemployment problem, compared to recommendations to straight people. When a man rapes a woman, who identified with the victim and who with the rapist? Indicate the kind of victim whose victimization disturbs us least. [408-409]

9. Describe what Thornton (1992) revealed about repressors' and sensitizers' attributions to a rape victim. Define "social model." Describe the Bryan and Test (1967) "model of helping beside the road" study. Is Lassie a prosocial model for children? Compare Barney to Bevis and Butthead as prosocial models. What was Coles' advice regarding the development of moral intelligence in children. [409-412]

10. Indicate how researchers have put study participants into a positive emotional state. Consider Baron's demonstration that pleasant odors can create a positive affective state and more helping. Indicate when positive mood would interfere with helping and when it would promote helping. When does negative mood lead to helping? [412-414]

11. Is any act every truly altruistic? Know empathy's two components. Define "sympathetic feelings". Discuss the two "perspective taking" positions and the role of fantasy in perspective taking. Discuss the portion of empathy that is genetically and the portion that is environmentally determined. What (or whom) presses our empathy buttons? [414-418]

12. Discuss similarity of victims to self and similarity of an emergency to one suffered by oneself as factors in helping. Discuss need for approval and personality traits as helping determinants. How important are personality traits in influencing helping?[418]

13. Define the "altruistic personality" components that differentiate between helpers and non-helpers at an accident scene and helpers versus non-helpers of Nazi victims. Discuss the "ordinary person" who saved a girl from a fiery crash. Compare his stated reasons for helping with alternatives. Are Americans generous with their volunteer time? [418-420]

14. Apply the five steps to emergency helping to prosocial volunteering. Indicate how people react differently to others judged to be responsible versus not responsible for their AIDs infection. List five basic motives for volunteering to help AIDS victims. Compare "selfish" with "selfless" motivations to help AIDS victims. [421-422]

15. Relate generativity to altruism. Describe the commitment stories of high generative people. Discuss why men, generally lower in empathy, help more than women, generally higher in empathy. Explain men's motivations to help women after seeing an erotic tape. [423-425]

16. Who asks for help and who does not? Indicate what motivates not asking for help and how help receivers are viewed by self and others. Compare who we would rather help us with who we would not want to help us (and how we'd feel if helped by the latter). How does help from these two affect out future motivation to help? [425-427]

17. Compare the motive we attribute our own helpful behavior with the motive we attribute to others. According to Batson's empathy-altruism view, what outweighs what when people show altruistic behavior. Describe the study by the Batson group in which participants had an opportunity to take electric shocks in place of someone else. [427-430]

18. Contrast Batson's view with that of Cialdini. What does the latter argue has to be present if empathic concern is to increase helping? Explain why people may avoid whatever increases empathic concern. Indicate what Cialdini group found when they separated negative affect reduction from empathic feeling as determinants of helping. [430-432]

19. Discuss the achievement motivation aspect of the Smith group's (1998) empathic joy view. Describe how their study, which varied feedback about participants help effectiveness, supported their position. Describe the "helper's high". [432]

20. Discuss the "selfish gene" and Burnstein et al's (1994) assumption about helpful behavior among prehistoric humans. According to their view, we should help others as a function of what factor? Is there a gene for helping?. Describe genetically transmitted social abilities that may influence helping. [432-433]

There's More Than First Meets Your Eyes: Understanding Figures in Your Text

Turn to the figures in your text that are mentioned below and follow the discussion about how the figures can increase you understanding of research and theory.

1. Look at Figure 10.2 (p. 399) and the accompanying text. It is beautiful in its regularity. As the number of others available to help goes up, helping goes down and the time it takes to help goes up in straight-line fashion.

2. Figure 10.4 (p. 402) is another beautifully regular display of a relationship. Help is a direct, straight-line function of how much time one has to make an appointment.

3. Look at Figure 10.6 (p. 407) and the text that goes with it. What sticks out is that both men and women are unwilling to help a gay stranger: At most 35% helped the gay man. Were participants afraid of "getting involved" with a gay person? Note two gender differences: Men are more helpful and women a bit more open-minded.

4. Figure 10.8 (p. 410) is notable in that it reflects only one real big effect. High repressors may have disassociated themselves from the victim as reflected in low blaming of the victim. They may have been "saying" subvocally, "This has nothing to do with me."

5. Look at Figure 10.18 (p. 429) and the accompanying text. This simple figure is a nice summary of the rival attempts to explain prosocial behavior. It can be made even simpler by attending to the rightmost column. For each row, the rightmost box indicates "why" an individual provides help.

KEY TERMS: CONCEPTS YOU NEED TO UNDERSTAND

Write out the meaning of the following terms in your own words. Cover the right–hand portion of the exercise until you have finished, then check on the accuracy of your answers by comparing them with the definitions provided.

1. (pro)social model — a person who performs a socially meaningful (helpful) behavior for others to observe. [411]

2. altruism — Refers to unselfish concern for others. [414-415]

3. repression/sensitization — avoiding or denying a threat/focusing on a threat and trying to control it. [409-410]

4. diffusion of responsibility — The hypothesis that people spread the responsibility for helping around, so that the more people present in an emergency, the less responsibility each bears. [397]

5. bystander effect — Refers to the observation that the more people present in an emergency, the less the helping. [398]

6. pluralistic ignorance — The observation that people on the scene of an emergency will play it cool, pretending that nothing serious is happening, ensuring that each communicates to the other that the emergency is actually not a matter of concern. [403]

7. wrong number technique — Calling for help, getting the "wrong number," saying one has no more money, asking the recipient of the call to phone for help. [406]

8. emotional state — mood or affective state that accompanies good and bad events. [413]

9. empathy-altruism — Batson's idea that at least some prosocial behavior is motivated solely by the desire to help the recipient. [430]

10. negative state relief model — Proposes that individuals are motivated to help in order to relieve a negative emotional state. [431]

11. empathic-joy hypothesis — The hypothesis that prosocial behavior is motivated by the anticipation of the joy resulting from observing that someone else's needs are met. [431-432]

12. genetic determinism model — The idea that whether or not a person helps others is a function of how genetically similar they are to him or her (so that the propagation of her or his genes is maximized). [432]

MATCHING

Match each concept on the left side of the page with an identifying phrase, word or sentence on the right side of the page. The answers may be found after the WHAT'S WRONG HERE? section.

A. high empathy subject took the shock for another no matter what

___ 1. influences whether one asks for help

B. generativity

___ 2. enhancing the reproductive odds of anyone sharing genes

C. most threatening helper among siblings

___ 3. Batson's empathy and ease of exit study

D. likely rescuers of Nazi victims

___ 4. commitment to the well-being of future generations

E. maximizing inclusive fitness

___ 5. younger brother

F. feelings of competency

___ 6. empathic, believe in just world, socially responsible, internal locus of control, low egocentrism

WHAT'S WRONG HERE?

For each statement below indicate what needs to be changed in order to make the statement correct. You will find the answers at the end of the exercise, along with pages in the text where you can find more information.

1. The bystander effect is lessened if the bystanders are strangers.

2. Urban people, because they are used to emergencies, are more likely to help than rural people.

3. Thornton showed that repressors were more likely to blame the victim of a calamity than sensitizers.

4. Children who watched a "Lassie" rescue scene were less likely to comfort animals, because the scene made them think of heroes, not helping.

5. As one might guess, positive mood leads to increased prosocial behavior.

6. Also obvious is that negative mood reduces helping.

7. A man in a crowd of on-lookers expressed remorse because he failed to help a child trapped in a burning car.

8. If they had just watched an erotic tape, males helped a female stranger longer than if they had not watched the tape, probably because any kind of arousal increases helping.

9. High generative adults wrote stories reflecting low commitment, because they tend to generate self-interested outcomes.

10. Step three in the sequence leading to helping in an emergency is "Deciding to help."

11. Religious fundamentalists, because of their deep commitment to God, tend to help others regardless of race, religion, or national origin.

12. Sensitizers are more likely to forget details a threatening emergency because they need to protect against their tendency to blow things all out of proportion.

13. Men help more because they are more empathic.

MATCHING ANSWERS

3-A [430]; 4-B [423]; 5-C [426-427]; 6-D [419]; 2-E [432-433]; 1-F [425-426]

WHAT'S WRONG? ANSWERS

1. No, the bystander effect is lessened if the bystanders are friends. [403]
2. Actually they are less likely to help, because they are primed to not look at others lest they be overwhelmed by stimulus overload. [404-2]
3. No, its sensitizers who are more likely to blame the victim, because they don't deny like repressors. [409]
4. Actually, the children were more likely to provide comfort. [411]
5. Yes, but not always: only if the need is clear and there are no negative consequences will happy people help. [414]
6. Actually, it can be the other way around. People will help to reduce a negative mood state, if it not too intense, if the help need is obvious, and if helping will be fun. [414]
7. Actually, he was apparently alone and he helped. [420]
8. Sexual interest was the probable reason for helping. [425]
9. No, they wrote high commitment stories, because they are committed to the well-being of future generations. [423]
10. There 5 steps, steps three and four are taking responsibility and knowing what to do. [401-405]
11. No, they tend to help people who are similar to themselves and who are seen as not responsible for their calamity. 887-8]
12. No, it is repressors who forget because they are prone to not think about threatening situations. [408]
13. The reason they are more likely to help is that they are more likely to have the skills needed to succeed in helping. [423-425]

TRUE-FALSE

Indicate whether each of the following statements is true or false. If false, indicate why. Correct answers are found at the end of the exercise.

1. Placing coins and dollars in a collection box increases donations.

2. People are less likely to think they would help if the emergency is simply described for them than if they were actually present during the emergency.

3. When we judge a victim responsible for her or his calamity, we tend to help because he or she seems so hapless.

4. Apparently there is a gene for prosocial behavior.

5. Smith et al. (1989) "resolved" the altruism vs. empathic joy controversy by showing that empathic subjects helped only when they would get feedback concerning their help.

6. In the Good Samaritan study, seminary students, as one expect, were the exception to the rule that if you are in a hurry to get to an appointment, you do not stop to help.

7. "Genetic" theory predicts that we will help others as a function of how close they are genetically to us.

8. Researchers have used a comedy tape to create good mood in subjects of a helping study.

9. We tend to help people who are different from us and who have suffered a calamity different from our own, because we will get the most credit from such help.

10. When we help we tend to make positive attributions to ourselves, but when others help, our attributions to them are less positive.

11. The Cialdini team have found that sadness associated with a situation, not empathy for its victim, predicts helping and they pose that we help mostly if we are identified with the victim.

12. People like the challenge of a dangerous help-need-situation such as when they would be interfering in a family or lover's quarrel.

13. People are uninhibited in asking for help, because they will be seen as worthy humans if they receive help.

14. Women and the young are more likely to ask for help than men and the elderly.

TRUE-FALSE ANSWERS

1. True. [410]
2. False; the armchair response is likely to be based on "what a good person would do" and most of us think we are "good". [399-401]
3. False; if the victim is seen as responsible, we are off the hook and tend not to help. [407-408]
4. False; what we do inherit is a capacity to communicate our emotional states and to form social bonds. [433]
5. True. [432]
6. False; seminary students in a hurry were unlikely to help. [401]
7. True. [432-433]
8. True. [413]
9. We respond with empathy and are more likely to help people similar to us and who are suffering a calamity that is similar to one we have suffered. [418]
10. True; [428]
11. True; [430]
12. False; they tend to avoid such situations. [404-405]
13. False; people asking for help may be seen as incompetent, so help might be embarrassing and lower their self-esteem. [426]
14. True. [426]

FILL IN THE BLANKS: A GUIDED REVIEW

Mentally fill in each of the blanks in the following section while covering the answers in the margin. Check each answer against the answer in the margin by uncovering as you go along.

1. In the Darley and Latané seizure study _____ percent of subjects helped within one minute if they were the only witnesses.

   85% [398]

2. The first step in Darley's and Latané's decision stages leading to helping is _____ _____ _____.

   noticing the emergency [401]

3. The third step to helping is _____ _____, the fourth is ____ ____ ___ ____, and the fifth is ____ __ ___.

   assuming responsibility [404], knowing what to do, deciding to help [404-405]

4. The _____ ___ _ ___ also apply to volunteering one's time and money.

   five steps to helping [421]

5. Negative feelings associated with being helped may promote __ ___.

   self-help [426-427]

6. Besides personal values, desire to increase understanding, community concern, and personal development, people may help AIDS victims in order to enhance their _____.

   self-esteem [422]

7. That we help similar others because they have similar ___ may have been true of humans since prehistoric times.

   genes [432-433]

8. A big factor in helping others is whether we ___ them.

   like   [406]

MULTIPLE-CHOICE QUESTIONS: A PERSONAL QUIZ

After you have finished reading the chapter and done the other exercises in the STUDY GUIDE, take the quiz found below to test your knowledge. Indicate your answers by circling the letter of the chosen alternative. Check your answers against the answers provided at the end of the exercise.

1. In the "smoke study," what percent reacted to the smoke?
   a. 75%
   b. 38%
   c. 62%
   d. 85%

2. The bystander effect refers to
   a. inhibition of helping when there are several witnesses present during a calamity.
   b. indifference to the plight of someone in distress.
   c. the apathy shown by the victim of a calamity.
   d. the tendency for people to "kick someone when she or he is down."

3. What were the results of Darley's and Latané's seizure study?
   a. No one helped.
   b. The fewer the people present, the less the helping.
   c. The greatest helping occurred when the subject and one other person were present with the victim.
   d. Most helping occurred when subjects thought they were alone.

4. Diffusion of responsibility
   a. involves spreading the responsibility for helping from oneself to others present in an emergency.
   b. entails absorbing the responsibility to help from others present in an emergency.
   c. explains helping rather than not helping.
   d. operates only when there is a single witness to an emergency.

5. Who is most likely to help and not embarrass the victim?
   a. a person with a handicap
   b. a person with an altruistic personality
   c. a stranger to the victim who is dissimilar
   d. a person in a crowd of strangers

6. Which of the following is "nobody's business" and, thus, not likely subject to intervention?
   a. a fight between children
   b. a quarrel between a man and a woman who don't know each other
   c. a theft in one's own neighborhood
   d. a person assumed to be a parent beating on her/his child

7. Men are more likely to rape and women to be the victim. Who is most likely to blame the victim?
    a. females
    b. male
    c. neither more than the other
    d. sometimes one, sometimes the other, depending on circumstances

8. Bryan and Test (1967) found that a woman stranded by the road-side was more likely to be helped if
    a. the helper were a female
    b. there was a model of helping up the road from her
    c. she was accompanied by another woman
    d. she was accompanied by a man

9. According to Robert Coles, children learn moral intelligence
    a. by watching and listening to their parents
    b. from TV
    c. from their peers
    d. by learning a set of rules and regulations

10. As for the genetics of empathy
    a. there is no evidence bearing on the question
    b. twins studies provide some supportive evidence
    c. the available evidence is at best very unclear
    d. empathy tends to run in families

11. Who is most likely to help?
    a. middle-aged as opposed to elderly people
    b. those with internal locus of control
    c. people with a history of having their need for approval punished after helping
    d. people who have extended histories of working in the "physical danger" professions, such as fire-fighting

12. The basic idea of the negative state relief model is
    a. relieving a negative mood in the victim is why people help.
    b. emergency situations generate negative moods.
    c. individuals experiencing negative emotions are motivated to help in order to relieve their unpleasant state.
    d. victims in negative moods are helped less.

13. When Cialdini et al. (1987) compared sadness with empathy as sources of helping, they found
    a. the two states equally important.
    b. that empathy was more important.
    c. that it was impossible to untie the two states.
    d. that sadness was more important.

14. All of the following are traits of personality that may contribute to helping, except one. Which one is NOT a trait of personality that contributes to helping?
    a. need for approval
    b. interpersonal trust
    c. narcissism
    d. friendliness

15. Which of the following is the most important factor in helping behavior?
    a. a history of being in need of help
    b. ability to take the perspective of another person
    c. being big and strong
    d. having some kind of disability or other affliction

16. Whose murder was a stimulus for the early study of pro-social behavior?
    a. John F. Kennedy
    b. Franklin Roosevelt
    c. Kitty Genovese
    d. Katherine Hawkins

17. Who were the first researchers to come up with a viable theory of pro-social behavior?
    a. Darley and Latané
    b. Cialdini et al.
    c. Shotland et al.
    d. Snyder and Omoto

18. Who is most skeptical about "selfless" helping?
    a. Batson
    b. Snyder
    c. Baron
    d. Cialdini

19. Which is a part of the "helper's high?"
    a. warmth
    b. relaxation
    c. contemplation
    d. peak experience

20. Which is a involved in the "empathic joy" hypothesis?
    a. warmth
    b. peak experience
    c. feeling good about accomplishing something
    d. getting rid of a bad mood and putting someone else in a good mood

MULTIPLE CHOICE ANSWERS

1. b [403]	6. d [406]	11. b [419]	16. c [397]
2. a [398]	7. b [409]	12. c [431]	17. a [397]
3. d [398]	8. b [411]	13. d [431]	18. d [430-431]
4. a [397]	9. a [412]	14. c [419]	19. a [431]
5. c [426-427]	10. b [417]	15. b [416]	20. c [431]

IF YOU'D LIKE TO KNOW MORE: FURTHER SOURCES OF INFORMATION

MOTHER JONES (1996) magazine had an annual "top ten most altruistic" people. Now it's more often. Periodically MOTHER JONES spotlights the most courageous and self-sacrificing people they can find. These individuals are sticking their necks out for the environment, for human rights, and other worthy causes. Tune in to this interesting magazine.

Alter, J. (1995, Nov. 6). Next: "The Revolt of the Revolted." NEWSWEEK. Are people like former Education Secretary William Bennett altruistically sacrificing themselves on the alter of the mass media as they "protect" us from lewd and violent movies and "trash" TV? Or are they self-righteously trying to decide what is good for the rest of us? You decide.

Darley, J. M. & Latané, B. (1968, December). When Will People Help in a Crisis. PSYCHOLOGY TODAY, 14-18. This classic popular article lays out Latané's and Darley's theory of helping in the most understandable terms possible.

Hurley, D. & Allen, B. P. (1974). The Effect of Number of People Present in a Non-emergency Situation: The Superhighway vs. the Country Road. JOURNAL OF SOCIAL PSYCHOLOGY, 92, 27-29. In a short article, these researchers tell how they staged a "flat tire" help-needed situation both on a super-highway and on a country road. True to the bystander effect, there was more helping on the country road.

Mason, D. & Allen, B. P. (1976). The Bystander Effect as a Function of Ambiguity and Emergency Character. JOURNAL OF SOCIAL PSYCHOLOGY, 100, 145-146. A complicated study is concisely explained in a few pages. Emergency and non-emergency help-needed situations were staged on both a country road and on a super-highway. More help was received in emergencies, on the country road, and when the context was unambiguous.

McCarthy, P. (1987, July). Help in the Highway. PSYCHOLOGY TODAY, p. 12-13. This little article is an update on the "helping on the highway" studies done during the 1960s and the 1970s. It contains many interesting real life examples.

Winik, L. W. She's determined that everybody gets a chance. PARADE, Nov. 22, 1998. p. 12-15 Aida Alvarez knows what it's like to be the underdog. She's from the mean streets of Brooklyn where she literally had to fight gangs to get an education. Now she has turned prosocial behavior into an enterprise. As head of the Small Business Administration she champions business opportunities for people who cannot get ordinary financing to start their businesses.

Barker, M. Ken Benedict's second chance. READER'S DIGEST, May 1997, p. 107-125. In and out of trouble with the law, Ken Benedict was only 23, but headed no where. He was working on a prison inmate forestry crew when fire broke out in Northern California. There was no reason why Ken risked his life by repeatedly running into the blazing woods to rescue the family of Cynthia Salsbury. He just did it.

Chazin, Suzanne. How to raise polite kids in a rude world. READER'S DIGEST, March 1997, p. 28-41 Two sociopyshcological methods are among those offered to promote the development of politeness in children, a kind of moral intelligence. One of them is familiar: parents who are good models of politeness will have polite children. The other is a less familiar technique, prompt and praise. A parent who wished to induce her children to show respect and concern for their aunt first prompted: "I'd be really proud if you would shake your aunt's hand and pull out a chair for her." And when the children do as suggested, they are praised: "I was really proud when you shook your aunt's hand and pulled out a chair for her."

Aldrich, M. W. A good Samaritan story with a bleak '90s twist. ASSOCIATED PRESS (Peoria Journal Star, A15), Nov. 29, 1998. The quaint college town of Murfreesboro Tennessee was shaken by three year old run-a-way. Little Roy climbed out of a window and waddled toward Main street. A grandfather of eight saw him, but was afraid to intervene lest he be seen as an abductor. So he followed the boy in his truck instead, blocking intersections into which Roy ambled without hesitation. Finally, a woman understood the strange scene—boy followed by a slow moving truck—and intervened. Is potential danger to one's reputation more important than a child's safety.

Go to http://www.pubpol.duke.edu/centers/philvol/index.html   This page is devoted to the promotion of volunteerism and philantrophy. Through it one can volunteer and learn about conferences and research projects.

Go to http://www.igc.org/igc/issues/activis/or.html   Become an activist! No, it didn't all die with the '60s. There are people out there still trying to change the world for the better. Through this page you can join them.

Go to http://wwwuis.edu/~radpsy/   This page is for people who are associated with psychology in some way and want to move psychology, and the world, in a more humanitarian direction.

THINKING CRITICALLY ABOUT PRO-SOCIAL BEHAVIOR

1. Does it really seem likely that not one of 38 witnesses to Kitty Genovese's murder ever did anything? Let's examine the situation a little bit closer. Assume the following: 1) the 38 witnesses were divided into three groups; 2) the first group, awakened at the beginning of the attack, saw nothing but what must have looked like a lover's quarrel in which no one was hurt; 3) the second group saw Kitty stagger, but didn't see the assailant with Kitty, much less an attack; 4) the third group was Kitty's neighbors and friends who knew that Kitty was under attack. Now, which group was unlikely to have done anything and which group was likely to have done something to help Kitty? See Allen, B. P. SOCIAL BEHAVIOR. Nelson Hall, 1978 for more details.

2. What is the altruistic personality like? To put it another way, what kind of person is likely to help others in a unselfish, even self-sacrificing way? Take it from your own perspective. Think of someone you know who tends to help others, apparently without a thought of gaining personally in any way. Now, write down 10 personality traits or characteristics that aptly describe the altruistic person.

3. "Blaming the victim" sets the stage for not helping. Going beyond what is in the text, consider some other reasons why we tend to blame the victim. Here's a hint that will help in expanding on the text information concerning this issue: Who, when victimized, is most likely to be blamed for her/his own victimization? In other words, what kind or category of person is most likely to be blamed for her/his own victimization. Try not to limit yourself to one or two categories of persons.

4. When or under what circumstances are people reasonably likely to help, given that the need for help is clear and that helping does have negative consequences (regardless of mood)? That is, when are people likely to help under conditions that generally discourage helping? Think in terms of characteristics of the victim. What kind or category of victim might you help, even when the consequences of helping (possible embarrassment, possible danger to yourself upon helping) are very likely to be negative.

5. There is a difficult philosophical question that research seems unable to fully resolve: do people ever help for purely unselfish reasons or is "there something in it for them" whenever they help, something that is the "real" reason for helping? Try answering this truly tough question. Can you defend "people help for purely unselfish reasons" or do you come down on the side of "there's always something in it for them." Remember, the goal is to properly defend your choice.

11

AGGRESSION:
IT'S NATURE, CAUSES, AND CONTROL

CHAPTER OUTLINE: GETTING THE OVERALL PICTURE

Before reading the chapter, it may be helpful to examine the chapter outline. This will give you an idea of what is covered in the chapter and should help you organize your learning and review the material. You can also record notes on text sections under the outline headings for those sections.

I. Theoretical Perspectives on Aggression: In Search of the Roots of Violence

   A. Instinct Theories and the Role of Biological Factors: Are we Programmed for Violence?

   B. Drive Theories: The Motive to Harm Others

   C. Modern Theories of Aggression: Taking Account of Learning, Cognitions, Mood, and Arousal

II. Determinants of Human Aggression: Social, Personal, Situational

   A. Cornerstones of Social Psychology—The Buss Technique for Studying Physical Aggression: "Would You Electrocute a Stranger?" Revisited

   B. Social Determinants of Aggression: Frustration, Provocation, Media Violence, and Heightened Arousal

      1. Frustration: Why not getting what you want (or what you'd expect) can sometimes lead to aggression

      2. Direct provocation: When aggression breeds aggression

      3. Exposure to media violence: The effects of witnessing aggression

      4. Heightened arousal: Emotion, cognition, and aggression

      5. Sexual arousal and aggression: Are love and hate really two sides of the same behavioral coin?

C. Personal Causes of Aggression

   1. The Type A behavior pattern: Why the A in Type A could stand for aggression.

   2. Perceiving evil intent in others: Hostile attributional bias

   3. Diversity—Gender differences in aggression: Do they exist?

D. Beyond the Headlines: As Social Psychologists See it—Murder of the Truly Defenseless: When Mothers Go Berserk

E. Situational Determinants of Aggression: The effects of High Temperatures and Alcohol Consumption

   1. High temperatures and aggression: Does being hot really make us boil?

   2. Alcohol and aggression: A potentially dangerous mix

III. Child Abuse and Workplace Violence: Aggression in Long-Term Relationships

   A. Child Treatment: Harming the Innocent

      1. Familicide: Extreme violence within families

   B. Workplace Violence: Aggression on the Job

IV. Prevention and Control of Aggression: Some Useful Techniques

   A. Punishment: An Effective Deterrent to Violence?

   B. Catharsis: Does Getting It Out of Your System Really Help?

   C. Cognitive Interventions: Apologies and Overcoming Cognitive Deficits

   D. Other Techniques for Reducing Aggression: Exposure to Nonaggressive Models, Training in Social Skills, and Incompatible Responses

      1. Exposure to nonaggressive models: The contagion of restraint

      2. Training in social skills: Learning to get along with others

      3. Incompatible responses: People who feel good don't aggress

V. Social Diversity: A Critical Analysis "Would you murder someone you truly hated if you could get away with it ?" Cultural and Gender Differences in Aggressive Intentions

LEARNING OBJECTIVES: WHAT YOU SHOULD LEARN

As you are reading the chapter, these objectives provide page–by–page questions for you to answer. Answering the objectives should assure that you understand the essential material in the chapter.

1. Define aggression and discuss the instinct theories, including Freud's and Lorenz's points of view. Why should social psychologists doubt instinct theory? Describe the effects of serotonin and testosterone levels on aggression. [440-435]

2. Describe the drive theories and the frustration-aggression hypothesis. Discuss the General Affective Aggressive Model (GAAM). What are some input variables associated with this model? List and define some input variables associated with GAAM. [443-445]

3. How is aggression been most often studied and how do Arnold Buss and Stanley Milgram figure into a controversy over this most used technique? What is the evidence for the validity of this technique? [443-445]

4. How does the frustration-aggression hold up after many years of research? What is Berkowitz's alternative theory of the effects of frustration. When does frustration lead to aggression? Discuss the role of direct provocation, including the Chermack et al (1997) study. [447-449]

5. Discuss the short-term lab studies and the longitudinal studies of aggression's relation to media violence. How does the media generate aggression in viewers or listeners? Discuss the Drano murders and "desensitization." [450-451]

6. What primes hostile thoughts? Describe how heightened arousal relates to aggression. Discuss Zillmann's excitation transfer theory and the role of misattributing residual arousal. Describe how mild erotica lowers aggression and strong erotica raises aggression by reference to Zillmann's two-component model. [451-454]

7. How does crimes of passion and sexual jealousy relate to the two component theory? Describe the Types A and B personalities. How did Type A personality and testosterone levels influence aggression in the "trade shocks" experiment [454-455]

8. Compare Type As and Type Bs on hostile aggression and instrumental aggression. Who is more likely to be wife and child abusers, As or Bs? Discuss hostile intentions and hostile attributional bias with reference to the Dodge et al. (1990) convicted juveniles study. What is the role of narcissism in violence? [455-456]

9. Describe how the genders differ in aggressiveness differently across situations. What does strong provocation do to gender differences? Describe the different styles of aggression of males and females. What different forms of aggression do males and females show? [456-457]

10. Is horribly violent behavior better explained by reference to abnormality or social pressure? [457-458]

11. Describe the intuitive relationship between heat and aggression and your text author's (Baron) early heat and aggression research results. Discuss the negative affect escape model. Discuss what Anderson and colleagues found regarding the relationship between violent crime data and temperature. [458-460]

12. Discuss the crimes that were exceptions to the linear relationship between heat and violence. Discuss how Cohn & Rotton (1997) resolved differences in research results regarding heat and violence. Consider controversies as to where the heat-aggression curve turns down and what hot means at different locals. [460]

13. What factors exist in bars other than alcohol that influences aggressiveness? Describe how Pihl et al's research showed that alcohol erases the difference between high and low aggressors in aggressiveness. Discuss how these two groups changed in aggressiveness across no alcohol and alcohol conditions. [461-463]

14. Describe the forms of maltreatment of children. Are most abusers victims of abuse themselves? Discuss the three major factors in child abuse. Who is most likely to kill spouse and children, him or her? Describe what it is that men suspect of their wives that leads them to violence. Discuss familicide. [463-465]

15. Describe the typical workplace murder. Is this kind of murder common? Discuss the kind of workplace aggression that is most common. Describe the three categories of workplace aggression that text author Baron et al found (1998). Discuss the role of perceived unfairness in work aggression. [465-466]

16. Discuss the managerial steps that lead to anger on the part of employees. What are the conditions under which punishment is likely to deter aggression and violence? Are they met very often in reality? Discuss why capital punishment is unfair and why it is ineffective in deterring violence.[466-470]

17. Describe the reasons why catharsis does not work to deter aggression. If arousal is associated with aggressiveness and exercise lowers arousal, why would exercise not permanently relieve aggressive tendencies? Describe how aggressing may even raise aggressiveness. [470]

18. Explain how apologizing for aggression can lower the likelihood of retaliation. What can one do to reduce the cognitive deficits that accompany anger? Discuss how pre-attribution that others aggressive acts are unintentional can lower retaliatory aggression. [470-472]

19. Describe how nonaggressive models, training to bolster social skills, and the generation of responses incompatible with aggression lower its likelihood. Tell how mild erotica and empathy lower aggressiveness. [472-473]

20. Would you murder someone you truly hate if you could get by with it? Discuss gender, national and ethnic differences in responses to this question. Name some cultural and religious constraints against aggressiveness. [473]

There's More Than First Meets Your Eyes: Understanding Figures in Your Text

Turn to the figures in your text that are mentioned below and follow the discussion about how the figures can increase you understanding of research and theory.

1. Look at Figure 11.3 and the text material on GAAM (p. 444). First, the leftmost "input variables" involve factors external to the individual, while the rightmost variables are in the individual. However, both types of variables feed into Arousal, Affective States, and Aggressive Cognitions. In turn, these internal conditions all contribute to aggression.

2. Consider Figure 11.6 and the text material (p. 450). The blocks represent, left to right, repeated opportunities to shock the rival. Looking at the white bars, it is clear that low provocation condition participants do not increase the strength of their shocks over time. However, looking at the black bars, it is very clear that high provocation participants increased (left to right) the strength of the shocks over time.

3. Look at Figure 11.8 and the accompanying text (p. 453). A near miss in traffic would raise anyone's arousal. That arousal sticks around for awhile (residual) though one may not notice it after a time. Then the frustration at being delayed at the airport gate occurs. Aggression is likely to occur only if the individual (mis)attributes the arousal left over from the near miss to the gate delay (top right), not if it is correctly attributed to the near miss (bottom right).

4. Inspect figure 11.11 and read the text material about it (p. 461). This figure shows very clearly that when time of day during which violence occurs is taken into account violence increases with temperature only to a point: following the bars left to right, violence increases up to about 80 degrees, then drops off.

5. Consider figure 11.12 and the text discussion of it (p. 462). It indicates something rather counter-intuitive: Comparing the leftmost bars to the rightmost bars, it is obvious that high aggressors aggress more, but remarkably, a look at the rightmost bars reveals that alcohol actually makes high aggressors less aggressive than when they are sober, and about the same in aggressiveness as the intoxicated low aggressors.

6. Inspection of figure 11.14 reveals that 81% of workplace crimes are of a type (for example, robberies) that involve an outsider, not solely employees (p. 465).

KEY TERMS: CONCEPTS YOU NEED TO UNDERSTAND

Write out the meaning of the following terms in your own words. Cover the right–hand portion of the exercise until you have finished, then check on the accuracy of your answers by comparing them with the definitions provided.

1.	aggression	the intentional infliction of some type of harm upon others [440]
2.	instinct	people aggress because it is a part of their essential nature to do so [441]
3.	GAAM	aggression is triggered by input variables: aspects of the current situation or tendencies of the individual [443]
4.	Buss shock machine	the teacher shocks learner method of studying aggression [446]
5.	frustration-aggression	the theory that frustration always leads to aggression and aggression always stems from frustration [448]
6.	longitudinal studies	research in which information about the current level of aggressiveness of children is collected along with amount of violent TV watched and observations are repeated over time [451]
7.	desensitization effects	violent media presentations harden people to the pain and suffering of others [451]
8.	Excitation Transfer Theory	residual arousal left over from some prior activating event about which the person is no longer aware generates aggression [452]
9.	drive theories	aggression that stems from externally elicited motivation to harm others [443]
10.	Type A	an aggressive, competitive, irritable category of individuals [454]
11.	catharsis	the theory that blowing off steam through nonharmful activity lowers anger and also the tendency to aggress on a subsequent occasion [470]
12.	hostile attributional bias	the tendency to see hostile intent in others actions that are ambiguous [455]
13.	Type B	people who are not competitive, not "fighting the clock" and not prone to losing their tempers [454]
14.	incompatible responses	responses that compete with each other so that it is difficult to perform both at the same time (laugh and aggress) [472]

MATCHING:

Match each concept on the left side of the next page with an identifying phrase, word or sentence on the right side of the page. The answers may be found after the WHAT'S WRONG HERE? section.

A. Zillmann's account of why arousal yields aggression	___ 1. serotonin
B. participants in the typical aggression study	___ 2. short-term lab experiments
C. when frustration leads directly to aggression	___ 3. unjustified source of aggression
D. violent programs seen and measure of aggression occurs shortly thereafter	___ 4. aggression machine
E. violent media increases arousal and influences current affective state	___ 5. excitation transfer
F. basic apparatus of the typical aggression experiment	___ 6. teacher and learner
G. biochemistry linked to aggression	___ 7. two-component model

WHAT'S WRONG HERE?

For each statement below indicate what needs to be changed in order to make the statement correct. You will find the answers at the end of the exercise, along with pages in the text where you can find more information.

1. "Blowing off steam," for example, yelling at someone, seems to drain off aggression.

2. Having engaged in vigorous exercise reduces the subsequent probability of responding to provocation with aggression.

3. Threat of punishment may work to reduce aggressive tendencies, if the punishment is mild, immediate, unjust, and unlikely to occur.

4. Exposure to mild sexual stimulation (nudes) tends to increase the likelihood of aggression.

5. Frustration is an aversive, unpleasant experience; that is why, according to Berkowitz, we flee, not aggress, when it occurs.

6. Justified and legitimate frustration yields aggression.

7. One thing aggressive people have plenty of is social skills.

8. Apologizing for aggressing just makes the victim more likely to retaliate.

9. It is clear that people who resort to very violent behavior are abnormal.

10. It is now clear that rape is a sexual act.

11. Contrary to evidence from other divisions of psychology, "modeling" seems to be unimportant in human aggression.

12. Only if subjects are aware of their residual arousal does it raise their aggression.

13. It is a myth that women are less aggressive than men.

14. Hot is hot no matter where you are.

15. The three classes of variables that relate to child abuse create their tragic effects by lowering frustration, thus, making parents not care what happens to their children.

16. In the long term studies of media effects on aggression, it was shown that media effects are short-lived.

MATCHING ANSWERS

5-A [452-453]; 6-B [446]; 3-C [449]; 2-D [451]; 7-E [453]; 4-F [446]; 1-G [442-443]

WHAT'S WRONG HERE? ANSWERS

1. "Blowing off steam" generally doesn't work to lower aggression. [470]
2. It increases the probability. [452]
3. It's severe, immediate, just, and likely to occur. [469]
4. Mild erotica reduces aggression. [473]
5. The aversive, unpleasant aspects are the reason we aggress. [448-449]
6. It is illegitimate and unjustified that frustration that yields aggression. [449]
7. Social skills is what they often lack. [472]
8. Actual it lowers the likelihood of retaliation. [470]
9. No, it is not clear. Very strong social pressure may be a factor.[457-458]
10. No, it is considered an act of violence. [460]
11. Non-aggressive models reduce aggression. [472]
12. They must not be aware of their residual arousal if it is to have its effect. [452]
13. Women apparently do show direct, physical aggression less but more indirect aggression. [456-457]
14. Not so. It is different in Houston than in Seattle. [460]
15. No, they lead to frustration which, in turn, leads to abuse. [463-464]
16. Not so; real-life aggression can result from earlier exposure to media violence according to the longitudinal work by Eron colleagues. [451]

TRUE-FALSE:

Indicate whether each of the following statements is true or false. If false, indicate why. Correct answers are found at the end of the exercise.

1. With the use of an aggression machine, it is reasonable to assume that subjects are really showing aggression, because violent criminals select higher levels of shock than people not prone to violence.

2. As most people believe, there is considerable physical violence in the workplace.

3. The three factors that are targeted to lower abuse are sociocultural, care-givers, and children.

4. Killers of family members tend to be males.

5. Narcissistic people don't resort to violence.

6. It is a myth that media presentations tell people how to be violent and they copy what they see in the media.

7. The relationship between sexual arousal level and aggression is linear: the higher the arousal the greater the aggression.

8. Dodge and colleagues (1990) showed that violent juvenile criminals showed lower hostile attributional bias than others.

9. Text author Baron's early aggression studies showed that heat increased aggression, but only up to a point.

10. A cognitive deficit is an inability to effectively evaluate one's own actions that may accompany anger.

TRUE-FALSE ANSWERS

1. True. [447]
2. False; a recent survey reports it is low level. [465]
3. True. [463-464]
4. True. [464]
5. False. They can be aggressive. [456]
6. False. The Drano murders are an example of copycat murders. [451]
7. False; it is curvilinear, mild levels of arousal decrease aggression while high levels increase it. [453]
8. False. The showed more of this bias. [455]
9. True. [4592]
10. True. [471-472]

FILL IN THE BLANKS: A GUIDED REVIEW

Mentally fill in each of the blanks in the following section while covering the answers in the margin. Check each answer against the answer in the margin by uncovering as you go along.

1. Violence on TV _____ viewers.

   desensitizes [451]

2. Aggressive models are among the examples of _____ variables of the GAAM model.

   input [443]

3. Type As are _____ _____, _____ ___ _____, and _____ ___ _____.

   extremely competitive, always in a hurry, aggressive or irritable [454]

4. One factor in men's violence against their romantic partners is his suspicion that the partner has been _____.

   unfaithful [464]

5. Strong arousal can affect us cognitively by creating a _____ _____.

   cognitive deficit [471]

6. ____ _____ lowers or eliminates gender differences in aggressiveness.

   Strong provocation [456]

MULTIPLE–CHOICE QUESTIONS: A PERSONAL QUIZ

After you have finished reading the chapter and done the other exercises in the STUDY GUIDE, take the quiz found below to test your knowledge. Indicate your answers by circling the letter of the chosen alternative. Check your answers against the answers provided at the end of the exercise.

1. Aggression is
   a. any physical harm-doing.
   b. intentional or unintentional harm-doing.
   c. inflicting harm upon others.
   d. an attitude.

2. All of the following are theoretical perspectives on aggression that have been considered by researchers, except one. Which is the exception?
   a. personal
   b. social
   c. prevention and control
   d. intra-individual

3. Instinct theory of aggression suggests that people
   a. are unlikely to engage in aggression.
   b. fear aggression by instinct.
   c. are "programmed" for aggression.
   d. are primed to learn aggression.

4. Freud believed
    a. aggression results from the death instinct.
    b. aggression is learned.
    c. people always direct destruction toward the self.
    d. aggression is determined by external factors.

5. Drive theory postulates
    a. that aggression is determined completely by the genes.
    b. that external conditions arouse strong internal motives.
    c. that aggression is practiced because it has been adaptive in the history of the species.
    d. that internal forces, free of any external influences, determine aggression.

6. Frustration may enhance the likelihood of aggression if
    a. it is perceived as due to illegitimate sources.
    b. it is a frequent occurrence.
    c. it is experienced by a person with low ego-strength.
    d. it is an expected experience.

7. How have social psychologists solved the problem of studying aggression in the laboratory?
    a. They have used an "aggression machine."
    b. They have accepted the necessity of hurting subjects.
    c. They have resigned themselves to studying only verbal aggression.
    d. They have abandoned the laboratory study of aggression.

8. Baron and Bell's hypothesis that aggression increases up to high levels of heat and they drops off because it becomes so uncomfortable that people flee, is called
    a. excitation transfer theory
    b. the negative affect escape model
    c. the two component model
    d. the cognitive deficits theory

9. Initial work by Anderson and colleagues using actual crime statistics and temperature data for some large cities showed
    a. a curvilinear relationship between heat level and violence
    b. no relationship between heat level and violence
    c. the heat level and violence relationship formed a u-shaped curve
    d. a linear relationship between heat level and violence

10. Which of the following is NOT among the conditions that must be met if punishment is to deter aggression.
    a. it must follow the aggressive act closely in time
    b. it must be viewed as justified by recipients
    c. it must involve multiple punishments
    d. it must be strong.

11. Which of the following is an incompatible response that might reduce the aggressive response?
    a. hitting a punching bag
    b. watching someone else be aggressive
    c. thinking hostile thoughts about the person who has aggressed against oneself
    d. watching a funny movie

12. What is the problem with the frustration/aggression hypothesis?
    a. frustration always leads to aggression.
    b. frustration never leads to aggression.
    c. frustration only intensifies the aggression that is already present.
    d. frustration can lead to other than aggression.

13. Along with environmental and care-giver variables, what other variable figures into abuse?
    a. sexual
    b. the child
    c. high income level
    d. religious affiliation

14. Dodge and colleagues have located a kind of attributional bias in aggressive individuals. Which is it?
    a. hostile attributional bias
    b. attributing own hostility to others
    c. internalized attributional bias
    d. attributing weakness to others

15. Dodge and colleagues found _____ _____ to be related to hostile attributional bias.
    a. sexual promiscuity
    b. depression compulsivity
    c. violent crimes
    d. schizophrenia disposition

16. Researchers find which of the following circumstances most clearly determines the degree of sex difference on aggressiveness?
    a. whether strong provocation is present
    b. just about any circumstance
    c. when aggression is optional
    d. the age of subjects

17. Using the "the shock your contest rival" method, Chermack and colleagues (1997) found that participants
    a. were easier on their rivals than their rivals were on them
    b. were harder on their rivals than their rivals were on them
    c. how many opportunities participants had to shock their rivals had no effect on results
    d. the level of provocation had no effect on participants

18. Which of the following were among the findings of Pihl and colleagues (1997) when they investigated the effect of alcohol on the aggressiveness of high and low aggressive people?
    a. the aggression of high aggressives increased when they were intoxicated
    b. the aggressiveness level that participants brought to the experiment had no effect
    c. low aggressives increased their aggressiveness when they were intoxicated
    d. alcohol consumption had no effect on aggressiveness

19. Catharsis is
    a. turning inward.
    b. "doing your thing."
    c. irrelevant to aggression.
    d. "blowing off steam."

20. Why do social psychologists distrust the instinct theory of aggressive?
    a. ironically it is too social in nature
    b. it is unlikely that one factor, biology, is the whole story of aggression
    c. they just do not know any biology
    d. there is no evidence at all for this point of view

21. When Russell and Baenninger (1997) investigated willingness "to personally kill someone you knew and personally hated" in two countries they found
    a. no gender difference
    b. no national difference
    c. an ethnic/racial difference
    d. a slight national difference

22. Watching violent scenes may
    a. lower aggressive tendencies
    b. prime hostile thoughts
    c. no important effects
    d. raises or lowers aggression depending on age of the viewer

MULTIPLE CHOICE ANSWERS

1. c [440]	7. a [446]	13. b [464]	19. d [470]
2. d [441-445]	8. b [459]	14. a [455]	20. b [441]
3. c [471]	9. d [459-460]	15. c [456-457]	21. d [473]
4. a [441]	10. c [469]	16. a [456]	22. b [451-452]
5. b [443]	11. d [472-473]	17. b [449]	
6. a [449]	12. d [448]	18. c [462]	

IF YOU'D LIKE TO KNOW MORE: POPULAR AND INTERNET SOURCES

NEWSWEEK's (1996, Jan 2.) recap of 1995 is done with cartoons, many of which are hilarious. What is striking, however, is the predominance of violence in the cartoons: a man committing suicide with a sword, a child shouting about "slapping [someone] silly," the "B" word being used on women. Violence was truly a part of life in the first part of the 90s.

MONITOR OF THE AMERICAN PSYCHOLOGICAL ASSOCIATION (1995, Dec.). Violence is Sowing the Seeds for Educational, Emotional Setbacks, 6-7. Violence is more than a physical threat to poor and oppressed African American children. It is lowering their academic potential.

Ubell, E. (1990, Feb. 11). The Deadly Emotions. PARADE, 4-6. This article supports the notion that hostile people's hostility is worse for them than for their victims, but sounds an optimistic note: formerly hostile people can learn to be laid-back.

ASSOCIATED PRESS (1990, April 4). Illinois Psychiatrist Works Overtime Combating TV Violence. Champaign Illinois psychiatrist Thomas Radecki, founder of the National Coalition on Television Violence, is Freddy Krueger's number one enemy. He and a small group of "peaceniks" who work long hours for little pay are devoting their lives to fighting violence on TV and in the other media. They rate TV programs, movies, cartoons, and other media outlets that feature violence, publicize their views on such shows as "Larry King Live" and lobby to end violence in the Media.

Go to http://www.apa.org/pubinfo/violence.html for the latest on violence on TV, especially its effects on children.

Go to http://www.usdoj.gov/vawo/ for research on violence against women and much more... President Clinton's remarks on the subject.

Go to http://www.mincava.umn.edu/ for links to just about anything you want to know about violence against women.

SPORT ILLUSTRATED, Nov. 8, 1998, p. 87 graphically shows the effects of violence in hockey.

Allen, B. P. (2000). PERSONALITY THEORIES (3rd Ed.). Needham Heights, MA: Allyn and Bacon. Near the end of the chapter on Cattell and Eysenck, Eysenck's psychoticism scale is described. High scorers can be prone to violence. He describes an illustrative case, a 21-year-old British male who likes parties, partly because they provide excuses for violence.

THINKING CRITICALLY ABOUT AGGRESSION

1. What is aggression anyway? Sometimes we say that a good salesperson is "aggressive." Does that mean she/he tackles clients and forces them to buy? Of course not. Indicate what aggression is, as it is discussed in the text, and what it is not. More explicitly, differentiate it from competitiveness and assertiveness.

2. Aggressiveness in the workplace is more in focus now than ever before, regardless of whether it is actually more prevalent. As your text indicates, little of it is physical in nature. Most of it verbal or indirect, such as gossiping. An interesting question arises: how can women deal effectively with the aggressive atmosphere at work? If they are aggressing indirectly, is their method effective? Afterall, being aggressive at work may be thought of as a means of gaining power. If so, she needs to be effective in her attempts at aggression (remember we are assuming non-physical aggression). Given that the answer the answer to the second question above is "no", answer the first question for her.

3. Child abuse is now receiving a great deal of attention. Well it should, but do you get the impression that child abuse is currently more prevalent than in earlier times? Given that impression, is it accurate? Do you really believe that child abuse is more frequent today, or, for example, is it the case that talking about it and considering it in the media has just become more common. Think about reasons why child abuse may or may not be as frequent today as it was, say, during the last century. Will it remain at the current level in the next century?

4. Are acts of seemingly senseless, multiple victim violence on the rise? Are acts like that in Oklahoma City, Columbine High School, Colorado, and in the Dunblane, Scotland elementary school more likely than in the past? Think about why these acts may have become more probable. You could take the difficult side: maybe such acts are not more probable; rather, the absolute number of mass murders has increased, but in proportion to the greater human population of today, they are not more likely. Or indicate why you think such acts are, in fact, more likely today.

5. You have read about methods for studying aggression: for example, the teacher-learning (shock machine) method and competitive game, loser-receives-a-shock method. How else might aggression be studied? It would be useful if there were more evidence involving real life aggression. Some such work has been done: for example, fighting on the school ground has been the object of study. Devise a procedure for studying aggression in real life. Come up with a way to measure a form of aggression that occurs in real life. Why would your method provide more useful information than the teacher-learner method?

12 GROUPS AND INDIVIDUALS:
THE CONSEQUENCES OF BELONGING

CHAPTER OUTLINE: GETTING THE OVERALL PICTURE:

Before reading the chapter, it may be helpful to examine the chapter outline. This will give you an idea of what is covered in the chapter and should help you organize your learning and review the material. You can also record notes on text sections under the outline headings for those sections.

I.   Groups: Their Nature and Function

    A. Group Formation: Why Do People Join Groups?

    B. How Groups Function: Roles, Status, Norms and Cohesiveness

       1. Roles: Differentiation of Functions within Groups

       2. Status: The Prestige of Various Roles

       3. Norms: The Rules of the Game

       4. Cohesiveness: The Force that Binds

II. How Groups Affect Individual Performance: Facilitation or Social Loafing?

    A. Social Facilitation: Performance in the Presence of Others

       1. The Presence of Others: Is It Always Facilitating?

       2. The Drive Theory of Social Facilitation: Other Persons as a Source of Arousal

       3. Distraction–Conflict Theory: A Possible Resolution

    B. Cornerstones of Social Psychology: Performance in the Presence of Others: The Simplest Group Effect

    C. Social Loafing: Letting Others Do the Work When Part of a Group

C. Potential Dangers of Group Decision Making: Groupthink and the Tendency of Group Members to Tell Each Other What They Already Know

1. Groupthink: When Too Much Cohesiveness Is a Dangerous Thing

2. Why Groups Often Fail to Share Information Available to Some, but Not All, of Their Members

LEARNING OBJECTIVES: WHAT YOU SHOULD LEARN

As you are reading the chapter, these objectives provide page–by–page questions for you to answer. Answering the objectives should assure that you understand the essential material in the chapter.

1. Examine the text's definition of a group, and know the five key aspects of the definition. [480-481]

2. List the five reasons people join groups. [482]

3. Describe how groups benefit by having different members fulfill different roles, and indicate how internalized roles and role conflict can sometimes be detrimental to group functioning. [483]

4. Describe how one's status in a group and adherence to the group's norms are related to outcomes received. [483-484]

5. Define cohesiveness and list factors that contribute to group cohesiveness. [484]

6. In Allport's classic research, how did the presence of others affect performance on a word association task as well as on more complex thinking tasks? [485-487]

7. Explain how Zajonc's drive theory resolves the "puzzle" created by the fact that performance is sometimes improved by an audience and sometimes impaired. [487-489]

8. Distinguish between the mere physical presence hypothesis, the evaluation apprehension hypothesis, and distraction-conflict theory, and describe research findings that support each view. [489-490]

9. Give examples of tasks that often produce social loafing, and summarize explanations for social loafing. [490-491]

10. How do expectancy, instrumentality, and valence work to produce social loafing? [491-492]

11. Understand the five techniques that can be used to reduce social loafing. [492-493]

12. Describe the nature of cooperation and conflict and indicate how mixed motives created by social dilemmas often tempt individuals to defect from cooperation. [494-496]

13. How does reciprocity affect our willingness to cooperate? [496-497]

14. Examine the effects of positive vs. negative framing on the cooperation shown by cooperative persons, individualistic persons, and competitive persons. [497-498]

15. When does communication lead to a decrease in cooperation, and under what circumstances does it lead to an increase in cooperation? [498-499]

16. Know the text's definition of conflict and understand the four major social causes of conflict. [499-501]

17. What happened when the chairman of Delta Air Lines said "So be it!" in response to dissatisfaction among company employees? [501-502]

18. Explain how each of the following might be used/misused to increase a bargainer's success: a) the opponent's aspirations; b) common-value issues; c) integrative agreements; d) an understanding of bargainers' perceptual errors; and e) superordinate goals. [502-506]

19. Compare the focus of individuals who experience conflicts with members of their own cultural or ethnic groups with the focus of individuals who experience conflicts with persons from other groups. [506-507]

20. Describe how contributions and outcomes must be distributed among group members in order for distributive justice to exist, and how does self-serving bias affect our perceptions? [508-509]

22. Describe procedural and interpersonal justice, along with the factors that lead us to perceive that these conditions exist.[509-510]

23. Summarize strategies to "restore justice" used by persons who feel they've been treated unfairly. [510-512]

24. How can social decision schemes be used to predict group decisions? [513]

25. Distinguish between normative and informational influence and indicate when each of these types of influence tends to be preferred. [513-514]

26. Describe group polarization in decision-making groups, and explain group polarization in terms of social comparison, the arguments presented during discussion, and social decision schemes. [514-515]

27. What is groupthink, and how is it related to group cohesiveness, emergent group norms, and concurrence seeking? [516]

28. Why does the hoped-for advantage of pooling resources often fail to occur in group discussions, and what can groups do to counter their tendency to ignore unshared information? [516-517]

There's More Than First Meets Your Eyes: Understanding Figures in Your Text

Turn to the figures in your text that are mentioned below and follow the discussion about how the figures can increase you understanding of research and theory.

1. Figure 12.6 (page 488) summarizes the well-known drive theory of social facilitation presented by Robert Zajonc in 1965. The theory summarizes the circumstances under which the presence of others leads to enhanced performance and the circumstances under which it leads to impaired performance. Be sure you understand this important figure.

2. Figure 12.11 (page 498) presents a complicated picture. A way to summarize it is to first compare cooperative and individualistic persons. Overall, cooperative persons cooperate more than individualists (no surprise!). Cooperative persons cooperate especially when they're in a negative frame (i.e., they're trying to avoid losses) and individualists cooperate least when in a negative frame. Competitive persons are a special case. They don't cooperate much in either the positive or negative framing condition.

KEY TERMS: CONCEPTS YOU NEED TO UNDERSTAND

Write out the meaning of the following terms in your own words. Cover the right–hand portion of the exercise until you have finished, then check on the accuracy of your answers by comparing them with the definitions provided.

1.	group	persons who interact, share common goals, are interdependent, and recognize that they belong to a group [480-481]
2.	cohesiveness	all the forces, such as attraction and desire for status, that cause members to remain a group [484]
3.	social facilitation	the effect on performance produced by the presence of others; performance is sometimes improved and sometimes impaired [487]
4.	social loafing	the tendency for people working collectively in groups to exert less effort than comparable persons working alone [491]
5.	distributive justice	exists when individuals believe they are receiving a share of available rewards proportionate to their contributions to the group [508]
6.	group polarization	shift to more extreme positions in group members' attitudes and opinions that occurs as a result of discussion [514]
7.	groupthink	tendency in highly cohesive groups with dynamic leaders to seek consensus so strongly that information inconsistent with their views is totally ignored [516]

MATCHING:

Match each concept on the left with an identifying phrase, word or sentence on the right. The answers follow the WHAT'S WRONG HERE? section.

A.	concurrence seeking	__ 1.	members' contributions combined into single group output
B.	social dilemma	__ 2.	social loafing seldom seen here
C.	norm	__ 3.	situation eliciting mixed motives
D.	major cause of conflict	__ · 4.	tells members how to behave
E.	distributive justice	__ 5.	a characteristic of groupthink
F.	majority-wins rule	__ 6.	a social decision scheme
G.	additive task	__ 7.	faulty communication
H.	collectivistic cultures	__ 8.	members' contributions and outcomes in balance

WHAT'S WRONG HERE?

For each statement below indicate what needs to be changed in order to make the statement correct. You will find the answers at the end of the exercise, along with pages in the text where you can find more information.

1. The early experiments which asked subjects to think of as many associated words as they could in response to a presented word found that the presence of others caused subjects to think of fewer words.

2. As it is currently used, the term "social facilitation" refers to situations where improved performance occurs in the presence of others.

3. In any given situation, the dominant response is always the correct response.

4. The presence of others improves performance in situations where the person's dominant response is an error.

5. Social facilitation results occur only in the human species.

6. When students cheered as loudly as possible and the output of each individual could not be individually identified, the amount of noise generated per person was greatest in the large groups.

7. People who approach a situation with a negative frame are generally more willing to cooperate than people who approach the same situation with a positive frame.

8. If people imagined themselves as workers in a department that had received 70% of the company's bonus funds while "deserving" only 50%, they would immediately perceive this to be unfair.

9. The rule of distributive justice says that the primary factor determining whether someone feels he was treated fairly in a group is the considerateness and courtesy shown by reward allocators.

10. The factors determining whether we'll feel a sense of interpersonal justice following a reward allocation include consistency of the procedures followed, accurate information being used, and an opportunity to correct any errors.

11. When feelings of unfairness center around concerns about distributive justice, the individual involved will probably engage in covert actions (such as employee theft) to even the score.

12. The social decision scheme that serves to strengthen the initially most popular view is the truth–wins rule.

13. When people discuss their opinions before making a decision, the effect is usually to make them more moderate in their views.

14. There is no difference between collectivistic and individualistic cultures in the frequency of social loafing.

MATCHING ANSWERS:

1–G [491]; 2–H [491]; 3–B [495]; 4–C [484]; 5–A [516]; 6–F [513]; 7–D [500]; 8–E [508]

WHAT'S WRONG HERE? ANSWERS:

1. The presence of others caused most participants to produce more associations. [486-487]
2. Social facilitation refers to both patterns of results; thus it includes decreases and increases in performance. [487]
3. The dominant response is the strongest response that an organism has to a situation, and it can be correct or incorrect. [488]
4. Impaired performance is expected when an error tendency is dominant, improved performance when a correct response is dominant. [488]
5. Social facilitation has been demonstrated in many species. [489]
6. People generated more noise when alone, i.e., there was social loafing in groups. [491]
7. The negative frame seems to increase cooperation only among those individuals who have a cooperative personal orientation. [498]
8. When unfair distributions favor one's own department, people are relatively less sensitive to the unfairness. [508-509]
9. Distributive justice is determined solely by outcomes received. Considerateness and courtesy affect interpersonal justice. [508]
10. The factors listed determine our sense of procedural justice. [509]
11. Covert actions seem to be triggered by concerns about procedural or interpersonal justice. [510-511]
12. The majority–wins rule strengthens the most popular view. [513]

13. Discussion generally causes people to become more extreme. [514]
14. Social loafing is less likely in collectivistic cultures. [491]

TRUE–FALSE:

Indicate whether each of the following statements is true or false. If false, indicate why. Correct answers are found at the end of the exercise.

1. For a collection of individuals to be considered a group, the persons involved must share common goals and be interdependent.

2. The evaluation apprehension hypothesis predicts social facilitation of a subject's performance even when the subject is performing in the presence of persons who cannot observe the performance.

3. The occurrence of social facilitation effects in insects supports the evaluation apprehension hypothesis.

4. One factor causing social loafing is the fact that people in groups have less expectation that their own individual effort will lead to better performance.

5. Social loafing is enhanced when people work on tasks they find uninspiring and when they work with others they don't respect or don't like very well.

6. Social loafing is enhanced when individuals believe their contribution to the group merely duplicates the contributions of others.

7. One way to reduce social loafing is to make the contribution of each member readily identifiable.

8. Individuals whose primary focus is on maximizing their own outcomes have a competitive orientation.

9. An individual whose personal orientation disposes her toward maximizing her own outcomes while reducing the outcomes of others has an individualistic orientation.

10. Research results show that communication of any type, even faulty communication, increases cooperation.

11. When feelings of unfairness center around concerns about distributive justice, the individual involved will probably focus on changing the balance between their contributions and outcomes.

12. Research on distributive justice has found that we are more upset upon receiving more than we deserve than upon receiving less than we deserve.

13. Current research concludes that when group members engage in discussion, the members typically show a polarization effect.

14. The text concludes that the social comparison explanation for group polarization is incorrect.

15. When group members discuss shared information at the expense of unshared information, they usually reach final decisions that are of better quality.

16. One way to counter the tendency of groups to discuss shared information at the expense of unshared information is to tell them there is a correct solution and that their task is to find it.

TRUE–FALSE ANSWERS:

1. True. [480-481]
2. False; according to this hypothesis, there is social facilitation only when observers can attend to the performance. [489]
3. False; since evaluation apprehension is unique to humans, social facilitation should only occur in humans according to this view. [489]
4. True. [492]
5. True. [492-493]
6. True. [492-493]
7. True. [493]
8. False; this describes an individualistic orientation. [497]
9. False; this person has a competitive orientation. [497]
10. False; communication from others that angers or annoys often leaves the recipient hungry for revenge. [500]
11. True. [510]
12. False; we are more sensitive to receiving less than we deserve. [508-509]
13. True. [460]
14. False; both the arguments presented during discussion and social comparison seem to play a role. [514-515]
15. False; excluding unique information held by few members often reduces the quality of the final decision. [517]
16. True. [517]

FILL IN THE BLANKS: A GUIDED REVIEW

Mentally fill in each of the blanks in the following section while covering the answers in the margin. Check each answer against the answer in the margin by uncovering as you go along.

1. Different members of a group perform different tasks and are expected to accomplish different things for the group. In other words, these different members occupy different _____.   roles [483]

2. If a person occupies a position of high social standing or high rank within a group, this person has high _____.   status [483]

3. The rules within a group telling members how they should behave are _____.

norms [484]

4. When group members like each other, want to stay in the group, and are united in pursuit of the group's goals, the group is said to be high in _____.

cohesiveness [484]

5. The area of research that studies how performance is affected by the presence of others is _____.

social facilitation [485-487]

6. According to the _____ theory of social facilitation, the presence of others increases arousal, which in turn enhances the tendency to perform _____ responses.

drive; dominant [488]

7. When an individual's dominant responses in a given situation are correct responses, the presence of an audience will _____ the individual's performance.

improve [488]

8. The notion that a concern over being evaluated by others causes an increase in arousal and in this way contributes to social facilitation constitutes the _____ hypothesis.

evaluation apprehension [489]

9. The _____ theory explains social facilitation results by assuming that the conflict between attending to the task vs. attending to the audience produces heightened arousal.

distraction-conflict [489-490]

10. The social facilitation theory best able to account for both human and animal results is _____.

distraction-conflict [489-490]

11. Tasks for which the group's final product is the sum of individual member efforts are known as _____ tasks.

additive [491]

12. The tendency of individuals performing a task to exert less effort when they work together with others than when they work alone is known as _____.

social loafing [491]

13. The viewpoint which explains social loafing by assuming that people in a group don't see the connection between how hard they work and the group's outcome is the _____ model.

collective effort [491-492]

14. Situations in which group members work together for their mutual benefit are referred to as _____.

cooperation [494]

15. Situations in which one individual perceives that others have taken actions incompatible with his/her interests involve _____.

conflict [494; 499]

16. The strategy for resolving conflicts in which opposing sides exchange offers and concessions in order to attain a solution acceptable to both sides is _____.

bargaining [502]

17. Goals that are sought by both sides in a conflict and as such can serve to tie together the interests of conflicting groups are called _____ goals.

superordinate [505]

18. When available rewards are divided fairly among group members, according to what each has contributed to the group, _____ exists.

distributive justice [508]

19. When individuals perceive that procedures used to divide up rewards in their group were fair and that the procedures were applied in the same manner with everyone, they perceive that _____ exists.

procedural justice [509]

20. When individuals perceive that they were treated with considerateness and courtesy by the persons dividing available rewards in their group, they perceive that _____ exists.

interpersonal justice [509]

21. The tendency of group members who engage in a group discussion to shift to more extreme positions than the positions they held initially is known as _____.

group polarization [514]

22. The process by which group members gain an opportunity to determine whether their views are "above average" by comparing themselves to others during a discussion is the _____ process.

social comparison [514-515]

23. The tendency in cohesive groups to assume their decisions can't be wrong, that all members agree, and that contrary information should be ignored is known as _____.

groupthink [516]

24. Research suggests that, when it comes to pooling their resources, members of decision-making groups are more likely to discuss _____ than _____ information.

shared; unshared [516-517]

MULTIPLE–CHOICE QUESTIONS: A PERSONAL QUIZ

After you have finished reading the chapter and done the other exercises in the STUDY GUIDE, take the quiz found below to test your knowledge. Indicate your answers by circling the letter of the chosen alternative. Check your answers against the answers provided at the end of the exercise.

1. Research by Floyd Allport in the 1920s comparing research participants performing cognitive tasks in the presence of coactors versus those performing these tasks alone found that
   a. research participants working alone came up with more ideas, and ideas were generally better when alone.
   b. research participants working alone came up with more ideas, but the ideas were of poor quality.
   c. research participants working with coactors came up with more ideas, but the ideas were of poor quality.
   d. research participants working with coactors came up with more ideas, and ideas were generally better when together.

2. According to Zajonc's drive theory of social facilitation, the presence of others produces an increase in
   a. feelings of responsibility.
   b. diffusion of responsibility.
   c. arousal.
   d. empathy.

3. The evaluation apprehension hypothesis predicts that social facilitation of a performer's behavior will occur when the performer is observed by an audience that
   a. wears blindfolds and earplugs to keep them from observing the performer.
   b. is merely present.
   c. can observe and evaluate the performer.
   d. all of the above should produce the same level of social facilitation.

4. Which describes the social loafing phenomenon?
   a. When people are doing a task, they work harder when getting paid for it.
   b. When people are doing a task, they work harder when it's their own project rather than one they've been assigned.
   c. When people work together on a joint task, each member exerts less effort than when they work alone.
   d. When people are doing a task, they work harder when being watched.

5. Some researchers have led subjects to believe that their individual output will be recognized and rewarded, even when they are working in a group. Results indicated that
   a. social loafing was reduced under these conditions.
   b. social loafing was increased under these conditions.
   c. social loafing was unaffected by these conditions.
   d. subjects refused to believe that their individual output could be identified; thus, there were no meaningful results.

6. Judgments of distributive justice require that individuals perceive fairness in
   a. the procedures used to divide up rewards among group members.
   b. the considerateness and courtesy shown by parties who divide up available rewards.
   c. the ratio of contributions to outcomes for themselves and for others in the group.
   d. the outcomes they receive personally without regard to what others get.

7. An important factor in perceived fairness is the considerateness and courtesy shown to group members by those responsible for distributing available rewards. The type of justice described here is
   a. distributive justice.
   b. procedural justice.
   c. interpersonal justice.
   d. equity.

8. According to the rule of distributive justice, a common reaction by persons in a group who perceive they've received a lesser outcome than they deserve is
   a. to increase their contributions to the group.
   b. to decrease their contributions to the group.
   c. to seek smaller outcomes in the group.
   d. to examine their own outcomes without paying attention to others' outcomes.

9. Kelly, et al. (1998) had subjects try to come up with correct rankings of various topics during a group discussion. Under which condition were subjects especially likely to utilize informational social influence in the course of the group discussion?
   a. trying to rank leading causes of death under considerable time pressure
   b. trying to rank what people dream about under considerable time pressure
   c. trying to rank leading causes of death with plenty of time available
   d. trying to rank what people dream about with plenty of time available

10. Which social decision scheme suggests that the correct solution will ultimately be accepted by the group as its correctness is recognized by more and more members?
    a. the social-comparison rule.
    b. the truth-wins rule
    c. the majority-wins rule
    d. the first-shift rule

11. If a group composed of individuals who moderately approve of gambling get together to exchange their shared views, the group polarization hypothesis predicts that their views after the discussion will be
    a. more extreme than the views they initially held.
    b. less extreme than the views they initially held.
    c. no different than the views they initially held.
    d. split apart into opposing groups, some in favor of and some against gambling.

12. Which of the following is not a determinant of groupthink identified by Janis?
    a. leadership that is concerned with hearing all group members' views
    b. a high level of cohesiveness among group members
    c. pressure to maintain a high level of group consensus
    d. group norm keeps members from considering alternate courses of action

13. Social loafing seems to occur
    a. consistently across various kinds of cultures.
    b. in individualistic cultures but not in collectivistic cultures.
    c. in collectivistic cultures but not in individualistic cultures.
    d. among male subjects but not among female subjects.

14. Research on the pooling of information during group decision making suggests that group members are more likely to discuss
    a. shared information and that this tendency assures that groups will make good decisions.
    b. shared information and that this tendency often prevents them from reaching the best decision.
    c. unshared information and that this tendency assures that groups will make good decisions.
    d. unshared information and that this tendency often prevents them from reaching the best decision.

15. Which of these is associated with the tendency of group members to discuss information already shared by most of the group members?
    a. incompatibility error
    b. central processing
    c. hidden profile
    d. social comparison

16. Situations in which persons can enhance their own individual outcomes by acting in a particular way (except for the problem that all suffer diminished outcomes if many people act the same way!) are referred to as:
    a. social dilemmas.
    b. negative frames.
    c. reciprocal conflicts.
    d. incompatible bargains

17. The basic rule of social life suggesting that individuals tend to return the kind of treatment they have previously received from others is:
    a. cooperation.
    b. framing.
    c. distributive justice.
    d. reciprocity.

18. When people work with a partner in a situation that has been described to them as one in which there is the potential to accrue losses, which personal orientation is most strongly associated with cooperative behavior?
    a. an individualistic orientation
    b. a cooperative orientation
    c. a competitive orientation
    d. none of the above; personal orientation doesn't matter

19. Which of the following describes a negative frame?
    a. Someone threatens you as a way to increase cooperation.
    b. Someone makes a selfish choice in response to a cooperative overture.
    c. Someone cooperates with a partner, but the partner misinterprets the cooperative overture.
    d. Someone thinks about a situation in terms of the losses that could potentially happen there.

20. Which of these is not discussed in the text as a major cause of conflict?
    a. faulty attributions
    b. faulty communication
    c. naive realism
    d. negative framing

MULTIPLE-CHOICE ANSWERS

1. d [486-487]	6. c [508]	11. a [514]	16. a [495-496]
2. c [488]	7. c [509]	12. a [516]	17. d [496-497]
3. c [489]	8. b [510]	13. b [491]	18. b [497-498]
4. c [490-491]	9. c [513-514]	14. b [516-517]	19. d [497]
5. a [492]	10. b [513]	15. c [517]	20. d [500]

IF YOU'D LIKE TO KNOW MORE: FURTHER SOURCES OF INFORMATION

Janis, Irving L. (1971, November). Groupthink. PSYCHOLOGY TODAY, 5-6. Various high-level governmental decisions are analyzed in terms of "groupthink"—"a deterioration of mental efficiency, reality testing and moral judgment that results from ingroup pressures."

Colligan, M. J., and Stockton, W. (1978, June). The Mystery of Assembly-Line Hysteria. PSYCHOLOGY TODAY, 93-99. The interesting group phenomenon of mass psychogenic illness in industrial settings is discussed.

Burrows, W. E. (1982, November). Cockpit Encounters. PSYCHOLOGY TODAY, 43-47. What makes for efficient task performance by the small group working in the cockpit to fly an airplane?

Rice, B. (1976, January). Messiah from Korea. PSYCHOLOGY TODAY, 36-47. The basis of the appeal of cults is discussed. This article deals specifically with Sun Myung Moon's Unification Church.

Saks, M. (1976, January). Scientific Jury Selection: Social Scientists Can't Rig Juries. PSYCHOLOGY TODAY, 48-57. Helped by social scientists, defense attorneys picked juries that acquitted several famous defendants in the 1970s. Despite the cases, Saks concluded that the quality of the evidence, and not the characteristics of the jury, was the critical factor determining the outcome of these trials.

Go to http://www.vcu.edu/hasweb/group/gdynamic.htm This site is called the Group Dynamics Resource Page. It has multiple links to topics that have been studied by researchers studying groups.

Go to http://www.fastcompany.com/online/o2/meetings.html When people who work for an organization get together, it's called a meeting. You'll recognize some of the group processes discussed in chapter 12 in the "sins of deadly meetings" discussed at this site.

Go to http://www.influenceatwork.com/3victim.html Several pages at this site provide a thorough introduction to framing. Chapter 12 suggested that cooperative persons are especially cooperative in a negative frame, while individualists cooperate least in a negative frame. This Web site can help you understand why this is so.

THINKING CRITICALLY ABOUT GROUPS AND INDIVIDUALS

1. Chapter 12 begins with a discussion of what constitutes a group. A way to think about this issue is to consider various collections of individuals, trying to determine if they meet the definition of a "group."   Consider the following: 1) the passengers on an airliner; 2) the students taking your social psych course; 3) the members of a particular fraternity; 4) the "starting five" on a basketball team; and 5) all the students enrolled at your school. It's not so important that you decide "correctly" whether each of these is, in fact, a group but rather that you learn what constitutes a group by applying the definition.

2. Sports fans are well aware of the home court/home field advantage in competitive team sports. Playing at home is correlated with winning in baseball, basketball, football, and other sports as well. Social psychologists have tried to explain the home field advantage by using their systematic observation skills and by applying theoretical ideas developed in the course of their research. On the basis of their work, the social psychological journals contain several reported studies testing various hypotheses regarding the home field advantage. In basketball, for example, is it turnovers, crowd noise, familiarity of background cues, or the number of fouls called on the visiting team? To what degree are such group phenomena such as social facilitation, social loafing, audience effects, and coaction effects involved? These questions are still being debated.

3. Consider your experience in extracurricular activity groups. Can you think of examples in your own experience that illustrate social facilitation, social loafing, group polarization, or groupthink?

4. In the discussion of "fairness" it is noted that we are satisfied with a relationship to the degree rewards from a group match our inputs to the group. A question debated in social psychology is whether distributive justice predicts satisfaction in close relationships. Do we need to obtain relationship outcomes that are proportional to our inputs if the relationship is based on love? Or does true love mean that a person is concerned only with the partner's outcomes, without much concern over what they personally get from the relationship?

5. A study published in 1982 by Jackson and Padgett suggested evidence for a social loafing effect in songs written by John Lennon and Paul McCartney of the Beatles. The hypothesis was that songs written by Lennon and McCartney together would be of lower quality than songs written by either of them alone. Jackson and Padgett concluded that there is evidence of a social loafing effect, but only for songs written by them after 1967. (For a full report of the article, consult the PERSONALITY AND SOCIAL PSYCHOLOGY BULLETIN, 88, 672-677.) Can you think of instances where you worked on a group project and fell victim to a social loafing effect?

13

SOCIAL PSYCHOLOGY IN ACTION:
LEGAL, MEDICAL AND ORGANIZATIONAL APPLICATIONS

CHAPTER OUTLINE: GETTING THE OVERALL PICTURE

Before reading the chapter, it may be helpful to examine the chapter outline. This will give you an idea of what is covered in the chapter and should help you organize your learning and review the material. You can also record notes on text sections under the outline headings for those sections.

I. The Application of Social Psychology to Interpersonal Aspects of the Legal System

    A. Before the Trial Begins: Effects of Police Interrogation and Pretrial Publicity

        1. The widespread effects of police procedures

        2. Eliciting false confessions from the innocent

        3. Effects of the media on our perceptions of crime

        4. Effects of media coverage on perceptions of those suspected of wrongdoing

    B. The Testimony of Eyewitnesses: Problems and Solutions

        1. When witnesses are wrong

        2. Recovering forgotten memories of past events

        3. Increasing eyewitness accuracy

    C. The Effects of Attorneys and the Judges on the Verdict

        1. Attorneys: An adversarial battle to convince the jurors

        2. The judge's role: Enforcing rules and controlling bias

    D. Additional Influences on the Verdict: Defendant Characteristics and Juror Characteristics

        1. Social Diversity: A critical analysis—Race as a crucial factor in the court room

189

2. The appearance, gender, status, and behavior of defendants

3. Juror characteristics: Gender, beliefs, attitudes, and values

II.   Applying Social Psychology to Health-Related Behavior

A.   Processing Health-Related Information

1. Using health information

2. Beyond the Headlines: As Social Psychologists See It—What are the Effects of Vitamin C?

3. Accepting, rejecting, and acting on health information

B.   The Emotional and Physiological Effects of Stress

1. Illness as one consequence of stress

2. Individual differences in the effects of stress

C.   Coping with Stress

1. Increasing physical fitness to ward off the effects of stress

2. Coping strategies

3. Creating Positive affect to counteract the negative emotions aroused by stress

4. Seeking social support to cope with stressful events

5. Coping with the stress of illness and medical treatment

III.   Applying Social Psychology to the World of Work: Job Satisfaction, Helping, and Leadership

A.   Job Satisfaction: Attitudes about Work

1. Factors affecting job satisfaction

2. The effects of job satisfaction on task performance

B.   Organizational Citizenship Behavior: Prosocial Behavior at Work

1. The nature of prosocial behavior at work: Some basic forms

2. OCB: Its causes and effects

    C. Leadership: Patterns of influence within groups

       1. Who becomes a leader?: The role of traits and situations

       2. How leaders operate: Contrasting styles and approaches

       3. Cornerstones of social psychology: What style of leadership is best? Some early insights

       4. Charismatic leaders: Leaders who change the world

       5. The nature of charisma

LEARNING OBJECTIVES: WHAT YOU SHOULD LEARN

As you are reading the chapter, these objectives provide page–by–page questions for you to answer. Answering the objectives should assure that you understand the essential material in the chapter.

1. Define "forensic psychology," and describe the dimensions of interrogation and accompanying styles. Consider why people obey the law and compare the inquisitional interrogation approach (seeking the truth) with the adversarial approach. [525-527]

2. Discuss the ingratiational methods that are used to get the accused to feel comfortable about confessing. Consider the conditions under which an accused is likely to comply with law enforcement personnel's accusation that he or she is guilty. [527-528]

3. Describe the coercive methods that law enforcement personnel use to get confessions. Discuss the findings of Kassin and Kiechel (1996) who told experimental participants "whatever you do, don't press the 'ALT' key."[528-529]

4. What do media presentation on crime do to people's estimates of the frequency of particular types of crime? Describe the real crime rate as well as who is committing crimes and who are the victims. Discuss the legal assumptions we make when we learn that a person is accused of a crime. [529-532]

5. Discuss the sort of information about others that we are likely to weigh most heavily. Consider how "first impressions" matter in the way we perceive the accused. Describe the effect on the public of before-trial media information about the accused. [532]

6. Discuss weakening the effect of media information condemning the accused. Discuss presentation style of witnesses who are believed. Indicate when or under what conditions are witnesses likely to misidentify an accused. What is the single most frequent reason for convicting the innocent? [532-533]

7. Describe the relationship between the occurrence of misleading post (crime) event information and recollection of the crime event. Consider what may affect eyewitness testimony (Loftus, 1992). Consider Lindsay's (1993) assertion regarding whether false childhood memories are really believed by those who report them. [533]

8. List and discuss sources of inaccurate eyewitness accounts of a crime. Indicate which child characteristic and court circumstance makes children believable and who is most likely to believe child witnesses. Are children more vulnerable to suggestion? [533-534]

9. Describe the bizarre stories of "child sexual abuse." Discuss the need to investigate memories of childhood trauma that do not involve sex and gender and the call for criteria that discriminate between accurate and inaccurate memories. Describes the poles of the "repressed memory" debate.[535]

10. Do many psychotherapists willingly and knowingly suggest false memories to their patients? Describe the lost in the mall studies. Discuss why it is easier to implant false memories about the distant past. Does hypnosis increase memory accuracy? Explain why a line-up is like an experiment. Describe techniques that could increase witness accuracy. [535-538]

11. Contrast the stated and the actual reason for voir dire, examination of prospective jurors. Compare the ability of attorneys to that of college students in selecting jurors favorable to an assumed position. Discuss when leading questions can and cannot be used in court. [538-541]

12. Discuss the effectiveness of a judge's declaration that some evidence is "inadmissible": when may it be effective and when not. Does the emotional nature of inadmissible evidence have any effect? Describe the effect on jurors of a judge's unspoken bias in favor or against a defendant. Discuss the relative importance of race of the accused and of the jury and the wealth/celebrity status of the accused. Why do blacks and whites differ so on the fairness of our legal system? [538-541]

13. Consider the implications of the widespread practice of excluding Blacks from juries that deliberate the fate of Black defendants. Compare English common law with European civil law. Does attractiveness of the accused matter? Consider the effects of the accused's attractiveness and smiles on jurors. [541-542]

14. Discuss the accused's denial of crimes not among those with which he/she is charged. Contrast the verdicts offered by male and female jurors in cases of rape and child molestation. Discuss when jurors make up their minds and the effects of case complexity and juror competence. [542-543]

15. Describe "leniency bias" and "legal authoritarianism." Consider the odds of a guilty vote in a murder case when jurors against the death penalty are eliminated. Describe death penalty supporters. Who rejects insanity pleas? Describe a juror belief that affects her/his vote in a rape trial. [543]

16. Define "Health Psychology." Discuss the perceived "dangerousness" implied by the frequency with which the media reports cases of a particular disease. How should we regard the results of one small study that seems to have health advice implications? Describe the effects of scary health information. [543-547]

17. Consider the effects of positive/negative "framing" of health advice. Relate drinking and other risky behaviors to aggression and traditionalism. Indicate how social comparison underlies prototype adoption. Consider the meaning of "stress", how it relates to illness, and depression and the causes of stress. Can you catch a cold from stress? [547-549]

18. Indicate how Asian teens are the exception to the gender difference in stress experience that extends to physical effects. Relate social status to stress and illness and stress to physical symptoms. Discuss stress' direct and indirect effects on illness. Define psychoneuro-immunology, secretory immunoglobulin A, and catastrophizing. How does the latter and pessimism shortening life? [549-551]

19. Describe the implications of your initials. Do happy events yield happy mood? Contrast disease prone and healing personalities and relate the latter to "altruism" and secure attachment. Indicate how neurotics put themselves in harm's way and why Type As are disease prone. Discuss the health implications of eating well and exercising regularly. When do low-fit students visit the health center? [551-552]

20. List traits that promote fitness behavior. Indicate how to reduce negativity and gain control over threat. Define regulatory control and list the three beliefs that contribute to regulation of feelings. Why are counterfactual thinking and avoidant coping ineffective in dealing with stress? Consider "race" as a factor in the relationship between substance abuse and stress. [552-555]

21. Which affects stress more, positive or negative events? Describe the role of social support and secure attachment style in coping with stress. Which ethnic group shows high social support? Who gets support and who doesn't? Tell how disaster affects social support. Indicate the cost of supporting and getting support. Regarding hospital stays, indicate what is stressful and what lowers stress. Describe the importance of being in control and how socioeconomic status affects it. [555-558]

22. Define "industrial/organizational", "organizational behavior", "organizational citizenship behavior," "job satisfaction" (JS) and "organizational commitment." Indicate the typical level of JS and how dissonance explains it. List organizational and personal factors in JS. Who shows the most JS? Describe the role of the genes in JS. How stable is JS and how does it relate to job involvement? [559-561]

23. Relate JS to job performance. Discuss factors affecting the relationship between JS and performance issues and how JS relates to other issues. Relate organizational citizenship behavior (OCB) to the five actions that mediate pro-social behavior on the job. Discuss some factors promoting OCB. [561-564]

24. Relate the causal chain for organizational commitment, OCB, and prosocial behavior. What is leadership and what does it involve? List the traits of natural leaders. Are there many leader trait dimensions? Describe the results of the classic Lewin et al study of leadership style. Indicate how the Lewin styles are now broken down. Compare process and outcome directiveness. [564-569]

25. What did Peterson (1997) find regarding these types of directiveness? Discuss Charismatic leaders and the sources of their impact. Compare "vision" to "framing". List and define the personality traits of Charismatic leaders. [569-572]

There's More Than First Meets Your Eyes: Understanding Figures in Your Text

Turn to the figures in your text that are mentioned below and follow the discussion about how the figures can increase your understanding of research and theory.

1. Look at Figure 13.3 and the text material on compliance with pressure to make a false confession (p. 530). Pressure increased from left to right. With lowest pressure (slow pace, no witness) there was low compliance and no internalization or confabulation. As pressure increased, so did compliance. Essentially, internalization did not appear until the slow pace, false witness condition, but it went up when the pace quickened. Finally Confabulation was not a factor until pressure was maximum: fast pace, false witness.

2. Figure 13.7 and the accompanying text (p. 539) clearly shows the impact of a judge's unspoken opinion about the accused. When the judge believed that the defendant was guilty, he/she subtly communicated that disposition to the jurors and they voted 64 to 36 percent for "guilty." But when the judge believed in the defendant's innocence,3 the vote was split 50/50.

3. Look at the amazing Figure 13.8 (p. 541) and accompanying text. It clearly shows the rift between the opinions of blacks and whites regarding crimes where blacks and whites are involved. Notice that though both blacks and whites showed a relative uncertainty effect (middle bars) during the trial, whites perceptions of O. J. Simpson's guilt never got below 60%. Blacks also tended to see him as guilty before the trial (leftmost bars, 52%), but, perhaps in response to whites overwhelming belief in his guilt, never more than 18% of blacks believed in his guilt after the first trial was well under way.

4. Look at Figure 13.10 and the text relating to it (p. 550). It graphically shows how stress negatively affects both health and fitness behaviors that might starve off illness, thereby indirectly increasing the odds of illness. It also has direct negative effects on the stress victim's physiology. The result is an increased likelihood of illness.

5. Figure 13.11 and the text that goes with it (p. 562) nicely show the stability of job satisfaction and job involvement. For job satisfaction and job involvement when the job was similar at the two points in time, the correlation between scores at time one and at time two was about .47 (white bars; 1.00 is perfect). When the jobs were different at the two points in time, both correlated across time about .25.

6. Figure 13.19 dramatically shows (p. 571) that leaders' propensity to direct a group toward a goal was not important. Rather HOW they directed was very important. Regardless of whether leaders were high or low in outcome directiveness, if they used high process directiveness (insisting on hearing all views) they were rated high.

KEY TERMS: CONCEPTS YOU NEED TO UNDERSTAND

Write out the meaning of the following terms in your own words. Cover the right-hand portion of the exercise until you have finished, then check on the accuracy of your answers by comparing them with the definitions provided.

1. forensic psychology — psychology specifically concerned with legal issues [525]
2. inquisitorial approach — emphasizes search for the truth [526]
3. job satisfaction — attitudes concerning one's job or work [559]
4. psychoneuroimmunology — study of the interrelationship between stress, emotional and behavioral reactions and the immune system [549]
5. secretory immunoglobulin A — the body's primary defense against infections [549-550]
6. misleading post-event information — incorrect information presented about a crime after it has occurred that may contaminate witnesses recollections of the crime [533]
7. health psychology — focus on the psychological processes that affect the development, prevention, and treatment of physical illness [544]
8. industrial-organizational psychologists — psychologists who specialize in studying all aspects of behavior in work settings [559]
9. organizational citizenship — pro-social behavior occurring within an organization that may or may not be rewarded by the organization [563]
10. framing — leaders define goals for their group such that extra meaning and purpose is given to the goals and the actions needed to attain them [547-548]
11. stress — harmful and emotionally distressing responses elicited by physical and psychological events [548]
12. what is beautiful is good — the stereotype that beautiful people are also good (but, in fact, there is also evidence that "what is good is beautiful") [542]
13. leading question — a question designed to elicit a specific answer [539]
14. leniency bias — the assumption that the defendant is also a victim [543]
15. authoritarianism — the tendency to assume the defendant is responsible for the crime [543]

MATCHING:

Match each concept on the left side of the next page with an identifying phrase, word or sentence on the right side of the page. The answers may be found after the WHAT'S WRONG HERE? section.

A.   witness is self-assured, volunteers many details, and is not nervous
B.   catastrophizing
C.   dead heat in picking jurors
D.   stacking the verdict cards
E.   Type A

___ 1.   college students and attorneys
___ 2.   eliminating blacks from juries
___ 3.   competitive, angry, impatient
___ 4.   expecting repeated bad events
___ 5.   he/she is believed

WHAT'S WRONG HERE?

For each statement below indicate what needs to be changed in order to make the statement correct. You will find the answers on the next page, along with pages in the text where you can find more information.

1. One-at-a-time line-ups are proven worse than the usual line-up.

2. Jurors believe a judge's "ignore this evidence" most when police improperly obtain it.

3. Loftus' "lost in the mall" real-life study of an event that never happened showed that people's memories are not subject to false suggestions when real life, rather than lab, is studied.

4. The actual purpose of voie dire is to ensure that fair and impartial jurors are selected.

5. Social comparison processes interferes with the selection of a prototype as a model for one's own behavior.

6. You cannot catch a cold from stress.

7. Stone (1994) showed that negative events compromise the immune system more that positive events boost it.

8. Job satisfaction" pretty much is the same thing for everybody.

9. Charismatic leaders inspire distrust in followers.

10. In the classic Lewin, Lippit, and White (1939) study, boys with democratic leaders did not work well when their leaders were absent, relative to boys with other kinds of leaders.

11. Knowing what to expect of a medical procedure makes stress worse.

12. Trusting bosses and the organization is naive and leads to eventual low Organizational Citizenship behavior (OCB).

MATCHING ANSWERS

5-A, [533]; 4-B, [551]; 1-C, [537-538]; 2-D, [540-541]; 3-E, [551-552]

WHAT'S WRONG HERE? ANSWERS

1. No, there is at least some evidence that one-at-a-time is better. [537]
2. They are actually most likely to accept the judge's charge when the evidence is unreliable. [538]
3. Actually her study with colleagues showed the opposite. [535]
4. That is the stated purpose, but the actual purpose is to select jurors favorable to one's side. [537]
5. No, it facilitates prototype selection. [548]
6. Yes, you can, indirectly: stress compromises the immune system which makes one more susceptible to a virus. [549]
7. Stone actually showed that positive events boost the immune system more than negative events compromise it. [555]
8. Job satisfaction is actually "in the eye of the beholder". [561-562]
9. Actually, they inspire an enthusiasm and loyalty in followers. [571]
10. Not so. Followers of democratic leaders worked best in the absent of their leaders. [568-569]
11. Actually, knowing what to expect makes the stress less. [558]
12. Trust promotes OCB. [564]

TRUE-FALSE:

Indicate whether each of the following statements is true or false. If false, indicate why. Correct answers are found at the end of the exercise.

1. Social support makes people feel good, but it does not help them deal with illness.

2. As one might expect, being attractive was no more an asset for women than men defendants.

3. If inadmissible evidence is emotional in nature, it is more easily ignored by jurors.

4. It is impossible to train witnesses to be more accurate.

5. People may tend to report high job satisfaction because of the operation of cognitive dissonance.

6. In favor of a genetic explanation of job satisfaction (JS), Arvey and colleagues (1989) found that identical twins reared apart were more similar on JS than less related people.

7. Positively framed messages are best for facilitating preventive measures, but negatively framed messages work best for promoting detection behavior.

8. There is no such thing as a "disease prone personality".

9. Neurotics put themselves into stressful situations and they cope less well.

10. Ironically, people who are afraid of intimacy get much social support, primarily from "do-gooders".

TRUE-FALSE ANSWERS

1. False. It is critically important to health. [555-556]
2. False; when the crime is serious and the defendant is female, attractiveness matters. [542]
3. False. It is more likely to yield a guilty verdict. [538]
4. False; people informed that their first impression is best become more accurate. [537]
5. True. [560]
6. True. [561]
7. True. [547-548]
8. False. There is such a thing. [551]
9. True. [552]
10. False. They are, as intuition would have it, lacking in support. [556-557]

FILL IN THE BLANKS: A GUIDED REVIEW

Mentally fill in each of the blanks in the following section while covering the answers in the margin. Check each answer against the answer in the margin by uncovering as you go along.

1. Job satisfaction (JS) is high when workers are neither _____ nor _____.

   underloaded or overloaded [560]

2. Personal factors in JS include _____ and _____.

   seniority and status [561]

3. Little room for _____ _____ is a reason why JS and performance are only weakly correlated.

   performance variation [562

4. Martin Luther King's famous "_ ___ _ ___" quote is an example of vision in leadership.

   "I have a dream" [570-571]

5. _____ _____, _____, and _____ _____ _ _____ are organizational factors in job satisfaction.

   Reward system; fairness; trust in bosses [561-562]

6. According to Lindsay (1993), people who adopt false memories ____ _____ their false memories.

   actually believe [533]

7. ____ jurors acquit ____ defendants and white jurors ____ them.

   Black, black, convict [540-541]

8. Under European civil law, ordinary citizen jurors are replaced with _____ and _____ _____.

   professional non-professional judges [542]

MULTIPLE-CHOICE QUESTIONS: A PERSONAL QUIZ

After you have finished reading the chapter and done the other exercises in the STUDY GUIDE, take the quiz found below to test your knowledge. Indicate your answers by circling the letter of the chosen alternative. Check your answers against the answers provided at the end of the exercise.

1. Even the most honest, intelligence, and well-meaning citizens may make a mistake in _____
   _____.
   a. propaganda evaluation
   b. eyewitness identification
   c. union participation
   d. political acumen

2. Leading questions are
   a. never permitted
   b. permitted when the witness is first examined
   c. permitted upon cross-examination
   d. permitted throughout any trial

3. Jurors
   a. have proven as capable as trained professionally legally trained
   b. are rather universally incompetent
   c. tend to be highly educated
   d. tend to make up their minds quickly

4. Attorneys are very aware of a certain one of their biases during juror selection. Which of the following is that bias?
   a. racial
   b. gender
   c. attractiveness
   d. educational

5. Health psychology
   a. is a new field that looks at whether current theories are "philosophically healthy."
   b. is an ancient field—the one upon which psychology was founded—that is concerned with opposing domination by the medical community.
   c. is the field that studies the psychological processes affecting the development, prevention, and treatment of physical illness.
   d. is a new field, started by physicians, that seeks to unite medical and psychology personnel in the fight against disease.

6. Regarding ability to select jurors, research has shown that attorneys
   a. are better than non-attorneys.
   b. are uniformly skilled.
   c. are uniformly dismal.
   d. are no better than college students.

7. In terms of its effects on the public, media information
   a. has surprisingly few effects.
   b. tends to be most impactful when "negative" information is emphasized.
   c. tends to be most impactful when "positive" information is emphasized.
   d. tends to create irrevocable opinions about guilt or innocence.

8. When Brown (1991) looked at the behavior of undergraduates who were physically fit or not, what did he find?
   a. Fitness was not associated with health.
   b. Among students with high stress in their lives, those whose fitness was low visited the health center more than those whose fitness was high.
   c. Among students with low stress in their lives, those whose fitness was high visited the health center more than those whose fitness was low.
   d. Regardless of stress level, high fit students had fewer illnesses.

9. The "racial rift" associated with the O.J. trial
   a. Is overblown; there really isn't one.
   b. Is real; African-Americans and European-Americans saw the trial very differently.
   c. Is a matter of speculation; there is no survey evidence to confirm it.
   d. Was real, but as soon as the trial ended, the "rift" closed.

10. All of the following, except one, is a way to gain control over thinking and feeling. Which is nota way to gain this kind of control?
    a. regulatory control
    b. transcendental meditation
    c. trust chance
    d. separated one's emotions from the situation one is in

11. In terms of deciding on someone's guilt, we show a primacy effect: what we learn _____ about an accused tends to stick with us.
    a. last
    b. latest
    c. quickest
    d. first

12. The accused's compliance to police authority's demand that they confess is greatest when
    a. the accused is a female
    b. the authority figure is trusted
    c. when there is certainty about the right answers
    d. when there is an expectancy that the accused does not know the answer

13. Who is doing what to whom in terms of crime?
    a. middle aged men are the most likely criminals
    b. black on white crime is more frequent than black on black crime
    c. elderly people are the most likely crime victims
    d. young males on young males is the most likely crime scenario

14. In view of studies that show children are vulnerable to false memory transplantation and absurd stories of abuse by aliens and Satanic cults, Lindsay has called for
    a. banning of child witnesses
    b. investigations into cults
    c. means of differentiation between true and false memories
    d. coaching of child witnesses

15. Industrial-organizational psychology is
    a. a branch of business dominated by psychologists.
    b. a branch of psychology dominated by in business.
    c. a group of corporate attorneys interested in psychology.
    d. a branch of psychology that studies behavior in work settings.

16. Wells and Luus drew an analogy between a police identification lineup and
    a. a social psychology experiment
    b. gang fight
    c. a wrestling match
    d. a beauty contest

17. What do the genders differ on most?
    a. natural leadership ability
    b. support for life without parole
    c. tendency to be physically fit and psychological sound
    d. tendency to vote "guilty" in rape and child abuse cases

18. "Organizational citizenship behavior" promotes pro-social behavior on the job. What forms does prosocial behavior take?
    a. extraversion
    b. self-sacrifice
    c. thoughtfulness
    d. sportsmanship

19. The best way to ensure the death penalty is applied is to
    a. lodge it against a retarded accused
    b. get rid of anti-death penalty people from the potential jury pool
    c. get an all black jury
    d. carry on a campaign of leaks to the press and other new media outlets

20. Vitamin C is
    a. good for you
    b. bad for you
    c. good or bad, depending on the latest study results
    d. good or bad depending on results of many large scale studies

21. Drinking excessively and other reckless behavior goes along with which of the following?
   a. low traditionalism
   b. high harm avoidance
   c. sexual caution
   d. low violence

22. Cornary heart disease is most closely associated with which of the following?
   a. low self-esteem
   b. high socioeconomic level
   c. low social status
   d. high aspirations

23. Positive events, such as weddings,
   a. have universally positive effects
   b. have universally negative effects because they never measure up to expectations
   c. always have mixed positive and negative effects
   d. may have negative effects

MULTIPLE–CHOICE ANSWERS

1. b [533]	7. b [531]	13. d [530]	19. b [543]
2. c [538]	8. b [553]	14. c [535]	20. d [546]
3. d [542-543]	9. b [541]	15. d [559]	21. a [548]
4. a [541]	10. c [553]	16. a [536]	22. c.[549]
5. c [544]	11. d [531]	17. d [542]	23. d [551]
6. d [537-538]	12. b [528]	18. d [564]	

IF YOU'D LIKE TO KNOW MORE: FURTHER SOURCES OF INFORMATION

NEWSWEEK, (1995, Nov. 27). The Road Ahead, 58-61. Office dirty tricks? Need for negotiations? Job satisfaction? None are a problem for Bill Gates, perhaps the world's most successful business entrepreneur. So go out and buy his new semi-autobiography? Forget it, it's too long-winded. Read these relatively short articles and find out how he did it.

Ellsworth, P. (1985, July). Juries on Trial. PSYCHOLOGY TODAY, 44-46. A 1968 case is used to introduce the issue of "death-qualified" juries. The relationship between social psychological research and court cases since then is discussed.

Kaplan, S. M. (1985, July). Death, So Say We All. PSYCHOLOGY TODAY, 48-53. The author describes the emotional turmoil experienced by jurors who sat through a lengthy and traumatic trial that resulted in a death-sentence recommendation.

Go to http://som.binghamton.edu/leadership and you will find an international center for information on leadership: everything from connections to programs, research, publications and more.

Go to http://www.ccnet.com/~bluenote/ for all about industrial psychology. There are organizations to join and graduate schools to consider.

Go to http://www.pitt.edu./~tawst14/healthpsy.htm for information on health psychology. You can investigate careers, publications and much more.

Go to http://www.uis.edu/~fox/law/Welcome.html Dr. Dennis Fox's law page includes links to psychology and law research, reading lists, publications, and academic courses.

Go to http://psych-server.iastate.edu/faculty/gwells/homepage.htm for the most fascinating information about eyewitness identification.

Rogers, J. Beat the Crowd. *Worth*. (1998, Nov.). p. 61-63. This article might have been entitled "Join the Crowd." It is all about leaderlessness in the marketplace. Something happens— Amazon enters the book market via the Web—and everybody is smitten. They jump in and buy, until the new company is grossly overvalued. What to do? Rogers says become an independent agent or get out of business.

Dalin, Shera. They call it the pillow glow. Business Plus (Magazine of the ST. LOUIS POST-DISPATCH), Nov. 23, 1998, p. 10-11. This enterprising woman and her daughter, Karen Kowal and Nicole Lear McClain, make a sweet smelling, stress reducing neck pillow that can be microwaved for muscle tension relief, or cooled in the frig for migraine relief. Karen started by peddling her wares at conventions for older people. Now she and her national accounts manager daughter tout potential revenue of $300,000 for 1998. Being her own boss circumvents the respect problems many women face as executives in large companies.

THINKING CRITICALLY ABOUT LEGAL AND MEDICAL ISSUES AND ORGANIZATIONAL PSYCHOLOGY

1. Why do you think that "Court TV" has become so popular? Try to get beyond the obvious: famous recent trials such that of O.J., the mother who drowned her two boys, and the man who shot commuter train passengers and all the teenage boys who have used classmates for target practice. Could there be something more deep-seated here? Hint: is there a link between increased violence in the media, because of increased interest in violent portrayals, and the increased audiences for "Court TV?"

2. What do you think of the adversary system (each side does all it can to win, regardless of principles like "getting at the truth," "justice," and the "common good." Could you devise a system in which there is cooperation between prosecution and defense, between those who sue and those who are named in a suit? To make a possibly long answer short, just indicate the key ingredient in a cooperative system.

3. Besides those factors listed in the text, what conditions or circumstances do you think would contribute to job satisfaction? Here is an example: the widespread availability of unpaid leave for fathers who wish to spend time with their young children (with no bias against those who takesuch leaves in terms of promotion and evaluation considerations). Think of some new factors that would make job satisfaction greater for you and are likely not to have occurred to others.

4. Try out this strategy: write about your negative experiences. What has happened to you recently, or perhaps occurred in the past but is still on your mind, that constitutes an unresolved emotional trauma ("trauma" need not imply an extreme life event, such as a death in the family, or even the end of a romantic relationship). Pick one or more negative experiences and write at least a page describing it and your feelings about it. Feel better? Can you now resolve the conflicts surrounding it?

5. How much should you learn on your own about your medical conditions? With the internet and the World Wide Web available, it is possible to accumulate much seemingly useful information about various disorders and diseases. A friend, for example, found a medication that helped her husband's heart condition, a substance not mentioned by the cardiac specialists. But is this good strategy? Should one rely only on information provided directly by trained personnel who are familiar with one's disorders and diseases? List the benefits and dangers of self-acquired information.

6. Are there any greater leaders around today? In view of his troubles, Bill Clinton probably does not qualify. Why isn't Jesse Jackson the next Martin Luther King? Why has Newt Gingrich failed even to keep his position as speaker of the House, much less meet some people's great expectations for him? Do Al Gore's campaign finance problems render him dead in the political waters even before he can take the leader's oars, much less use them effectively? Where are you Harry Truman when we need you? It may well be that these leaderless times are, well, a sign of the times. Rather than no new leaders being born, maybe the problem is that we have grown cynical and cannot accept anyone as our leader. What do you think?

NOTES

NOTES

NOTES

NOTES

NOTES

NOTES

NOTES

NOTES

NOTES

NOTES

NOTES

NOTES

NOTES

NOTES